COI

G000139114

CATS

PHOTOGUIDE

Deborah Gill

Consultants:
Claire Bessant & Peter Neville

HarperCollins*Publishers*

HarperCollins Publishers
PO Box, Glasgow, G4 0NB

First published 1996

Reprint 9 8 7 6 5 4 3 2 1 0

ISBN 0 00 470972 1

Created and produced by Flame Tree Publishing, part of
The Foundry Creative Media Co. Ltd
The Long House, Antrobus Rd, Chiswick, London W4 5HY

Special thanks to John Dunne

Printed in Italy by Amadeus S.p.A.

Contents

Introduction

Not for cats the selfless obedience and desire to please manifest in dogs. Cats would like you to understand that they live with you by choice - theirs. Without effort they retain their independence while at the same time finding the household with the most suitable feeding arrangements, and within it the cosiest spot to sleep.

Dogs and cats are generally appreciated by different sorts of people: free spirits, artists, independent folk, all like cats; team players often prefer the company of dogs.

Out of doors cats live a fully adult life as wild creatures, hunting and socializing in feline terms. Once back in the home, the cat reverts immediately to a form of kittenhood, looking to humans for affection, reassurance and food. In exchange for simply existing as household pets, cats appear to have a secure place in our hearts, as we admire them for their relaxed bodies and ineffable attitudes. Cats have never been very much practical use to mankind – no protection role falls to them, no team work such as a police dog provides, no organized behaviour like that of a gun dog. Instead, their very presence calms and quietens.

Modern urban dwellers find a cat the perfect pet, clean in its habits, independent and inexpensive to keep. Older people, perhaps no longer capable of taking a dog for long daily walks, can find the ideal companion in a cat; a cat which will sleep peacefully on one's lap for hours at a time, providing warmth and solace.

Although cat breeding and showing are huge money-spinners, even the champion of champions at the most prestigious of cat shows is also a family pet, and loved as much for himself as for his ability to win prizes. Look carefully at your cat – with his graceful ways, he is the most fascinating of creatures.

How to Use this Book

This book details a wide variety of information about cats – everything from facts about breeds, life-cycle and breeding, to famous cat names, types of fur, and classification. A series of photographs illustrate each topic.

The book is divided into six sections, together with The Compendium at the end.

Each part is colour-coded for easy reference. Part One, which appears in soft green, presents general information about the genus felidae, the cat, including types of fur, anatomy and characteristics, and cat reproduction. Part Two is colour-coded pink, and provides information about cat habits, how they move, work and feed. Part Three discusses the non-pedigree cat, long and shorthaired, and is coded blue. Part Four discusses the pedigree cat. There is a special section on cat shows, and cats from North America, and here you'll find a discussion on unusual cats. Part Four is coded yellow. Part Five, coded lilac, presents an in-depth discussion of the shorthaired breeds. Part Six, coded a deep olive green, introduces the longhaired breeds.

Part Five and Six provide all the essential information you will need to know about breeds around the world. You'll find details of the breed's history and country of origin, and there is a 'Breed Basics' box which presents practical details of the cat: for example, its colours, coat length, characteristics and size. The Further Information section supplies interesting extra information about that breed, or simply cats in general.

The Compendium contains useful information on general aspects of cats, from caring for your cat through to catlore. There is also a handy list of addresses of various cat organizations, and a Glossary explaining terms which might be unfamiliar. At the end of the book you'll find an index which lists every subject and type of cat found in this book.

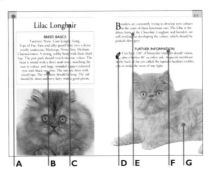

A The page number appears in a colour-coded box which indicates which part you are in.

B Breed Basics list all the important details about a breed.

C The title of the chapter, in this case the breed name, appears at the beginning of every new section.

D Wherever you see the cat icon you'll find feline facts of general interest.

E Essential information about the breed appears in a concise and fascinating introductory passage.

F Further Information provides interesting extra information about a breed or cats in general.

G The topic covered on this spread will be illustrated with clear photographs.

AN INTRODUCTION ≈ TO CATS ≈

Cats in History

The long-distant ancestors of the modern cat were the creodonts, small carnivorous mammals which appeared about 50 million years ago, at the evening of the age of the dinosaur. Creodonts gave way to miacids, meat-eating mammals with bigger brains whose descendants are the canids (including dogs), viverrids (including mongooses and civets) and the Pseudoailurus, the first true cat. These gave way in their turn to

animals like the Smilodon, a sabre-toothed feline whose fossilized remains have been found in North America; Megantereon, a similar cat found mainly in Northern India, Africa, and the Mediterranean; and the lions, cheetahs, and lynxes which roamed throughout Europe. From these came the African Wild Cat, from which it is believed our domestic cats are descended and still very closely related.

FELINE FACTS

• The first cats reported living alongside humans may have lived 8000 years ago in what is now southern Cyprus. In 1983 an archaeological dig at the Neolithic site of Khirokitia turned up a feline jawbone. There were no wild cats in Cyprus, so early settlers must have taken cats with them; it is unlikely that they would have taken a wild cat.

In 3000 BC Egyptian cats moved in to become pest controllers for the grain stores, and gradually the cat came to be worshipped as a deity. For about 1300 years cats were associated with the fertility goddess Bastet, and the severest of punishments was meted out to anyone who killed a cat. Cats, not useful in quite the same way as dogs for hunting or cattle for farming, came to live alongside humans in both temple complexes and towns.

FELINE FACTS

• Cats in ancient Egypt were treated to ceremonial mummification when they died. Even domestic cats were taken to the city of Bubastis, the centre of Bastet worship. There they were embalmed and buried, and sometimes ritually cremated. Many thousands of cat mummies have been excavated over the years: in 1889 19½ tons of cat mummies were shipped to Liverpool and auctioned off at £4 a ton for fertilizer.

• Egypt became a Roman province in 30 BC at the defeat of Cleopatra's forces. Phoenician traders took some of Egypt's previously closely guarded sacred cats back with them to Italy and elsewhere, perhaps even to Britain.

• The Romans took cats with them to northern Europe, and probably introduced them into Britain together with the first chickens.

Cats had a difficult time in medieval Britain and Europe. In religion they had been associated with the goddess of fertility and of virginity. In Egypt Bastet is shown with a cat and kittens; in Scandinavia Freya's chariot is pulled by black cats; in ancient Rome Diana is seen with a cat. Christianity overlaid the cult of Diana with that of the Virgin Mary, who is jointly the symbol of fertility and of virginity, and is often portrayed in medieval art with a cat. However, every faith which was not Christian was now deemed to be pagan, and as religious attitudes and social outlooks hardened, tolerance died. Cats, thought to be witches' familiars or incarnations of Satan, were burned in their thousands, and grievously tortured to make the Devil suffer.

FELINE FACTS.

• While cats were held in low esteem in the West, they had a better life in the Far East. They remained sacred in Japan, and were thought lucky all over the East. Many of today's breeds originated in the Far East.

• Today, North America is the main source of new breeds – from Ragdolls to Snowshoes, from the American Curl to the hairless Sphynx.

• In Islam, the cat is thought to be pure, and the dog adultered.

• Public attitudes to cats were changing by the mid-eighteenth century. In 1822 the first anti-cruelty law was passed in Britain, and in 1824 the organization which came to be called the RSPCA was formed.

• Today, as the world's most popular urban pet, the future of the domestic cat looks assured.

Types of Cats

Wild Cats

A ll cats share the same characteristics of self-reliance, agility, and strength. They are all superb hunters, with lightning-fast reactions and excellent eyesight. Only Australia and Antarctica have no native species of cat, and throughout the rest of the world wild cats can be found everywhere. There are 39 species in all. There are cats living in jungles, in deserts, on mountains, on open grassland and in the freezing forests of Siberia. There are cats who burrow, who climb, and who swim. Cats are carnivores, but if food is in short supply they are capable of eating whatever they can catch, and will even eat insects and vegetable matter.

FELINE FACTS

• The small cats (of the *Felis* genus), are able to purr as they exhale or as they inhale, but they cannot roar. The big cats, (largely of the *Panthera* genus) can only purr as they exhale, and are known better for their roar.
• The biggest of the big cats is the Siberian Tiger, which weighs about 383kg/845lb.
• Lions are the only cats who live in social groups, called prides. It is the lionesses who do most of the hunting in these groups.
• Tigers are the big cat most likely to turn man-eater.
• Many big cats, such as the snow leopard, have been

hunted almost to the verge of extinction for their beautiful pelts.
- There are 28 species of small wild cats.
- A type of wild cat with webbed front paws lives in Asia; these help it to swim and to catch fish.
- The Sand Cat of the Sahara lives out the heat of the day in its lair. It has thickly furred feet which act as protection against the heat of the sand.
- The Bobcat (which lives in North America) and the Lynx (which lives in Europe and Asia) are the only tailless wild cats.

Domestic Cats

Domestic cats today are of several types, according to the cat fancy. The Longhair breeds are recognized individually, and there are three types of coat: the Angora type, the northern cats and modern Persians. There are British Shorthair and American Shorthair breeds: many of them cobby bodied and well-rounded, probably from inter-breeding with heavy northern forest cats. Before the birth of Christ the ancestors of the Asian or Oriental cats travelled east from Egypt and Rome along the well-established trade routes between the Roman Empire and the Chinese Han Dynasty. Most new breeds are either colour variants of existing breeds, or unpredictable mutations, like Rex or Sphynx.

FELINE FACTS

• The Sphynx is one of the strangest of the new breeds, with its wrinkled, hairless skin, large ears, and anxious-looking face.

• The most popular breed of pedigree cat is the Longhair, or Persian, as it is called in the USA.

• The word for cat is similar in many languages, from the German *Katze* to the Spanish *gato*, and from the Polish *kot* to the Japanese *neko*. The root of the word may be the Arabic *quttah*, helping to link the origin of the cat itself to North Africa. Our word 'kitty' may have come from the Turkish name for a cat, 'kedi', and 'pussy' from the Egyptian goddess Pasht, or Bastet.

Types of Fur

Three different types of hair make up a cat's fur, but not all cats have all three kinds. The soft base coat is called down, the middle layer is called the awn, and the longest hairs are called guard hairs. In the wild, a cat's fur has many functions, but pedigree cats are bred for their looks only. In the case of the Sphynx, the awn and guard hairs have been bred right away, leaving the cat with only a light down.

FELINE FACTS

• A cat's fur provides wonderful insulation, and in the wild would adapt to suit the local climate. Even today many cats moult in the summer and grow extra fur in the winter.

• Fur also provides some protection against injury. It is sensitive to the touch, and supports the cat's scent, and so is important for identification to other cats.

• All cats are still hunters at heart, and the coat of wild cats is usually adapted to provide excellent camouflage for the environment they exploit (e.g., stripes in grassland or spots in a shady forest).

• The Longhair/Persian has the most luxuriant fur with the deepest down and longest guard hairs.

• The Angora has no undercoat, and its fur lies closely against its body.

• The Rex and the American Wirehair have down and awn hairs, but the hairs are distorted and extremely curly.

Coat Lengths

In the wild, the coat of a cat would evolve naturally to suit its life and the climate in which it lives. The original cats were probably all short haired, just as most wild cats are today – a short coat is a practical coat, needing little or no grooming. Long hair, together with a dense weatherproof under-coat, appears on wild cats living in areas such as Siberia. Modern breeds with their extreme coats, both short and long, have been bred to suit the tastes of humans. Many of them could not thrive without human protection. In fact many of them rely on humans to keep them warm or to groom their coats to reduce matting.

FELINE FACTS

• The modern breed with the longest hair is the Longhair/Persian, which can have guard hairs up to 12.7cm/5in long.

• The Persian-type cats shown at the very first cat shows looked very different from a modern Persian, with its very flat face.

• Wirehair cats have down, awn, and guard hairs, all short and curly.

• If pedigree cats were left to breed freely, within a very few generations their offspring would revert to wild.

Colourpoints

The basic cat colour is tabby, but sometimes a mutated gene can appear (called a mutant allele) which causes a differently-coloured kitten to be born. Where the tabby coat is flecked, and the hairs are banded with yellow, this is known as agouti. The black parts of the coat, with no yellow, are non-agouti. The agouti gene is dominant, and coat colour usually works on the principle of relevant dominance of gene: for example, if a tabby and a black cat are crossed, a kitten inheriting a pair of agouti genes will be tabby; a kitten inheriting one agouti gene and one non-agouti gene will also be tabby; but a kitten inheriting two non-agouti genes will be black.

FELINE FACTS

• Even self-colours are really tabby, but the non-agouti allele has removed the pale part of the tabby pattern.
• The blotched tabby, which probably first occurred in medieval England, is to be found everywhere in the world that the British colonized, taken as a pet and mouser.
• The mackerel, or striped, tabby, is usually found in areas such as Thailand, which the British Empire did not reach.
• The Abyssinian, with its handsome coat, is a full-agouti tabby.
• Genetics are better understood today, and breeding programmes are set up which aim to produce new colours and patterns. These can never be totally reliable, as nature is always capable of producing something unexpected.

• The colourpoints of the Siamese cat come about because there is reduced pigmentation in the hair fibres on the hotter parts of the body, and more pigmentation in areas where the skin is thinner and cooler: the face, ears, feet and tail.
• The effect of heat also makes Siamese colours more intense in cooler climates.

Anatomy and Characteristics

Even the most well bred cat is an expert hunter. All cats have highly sensitive powers of sight, hearing and smell, and astonishingly sharp reflexes. The skeleton is made up of about 250 bones (the tail has more or fewer bones depending on the breed) and 517 muscles. A cat's backbone is extremely flexible and strong, allowing controlled leaps and pounces. The intestine is short and simple as the cat eats mainly meat and is an obligate carnivore – eating plant matter requires a more complex digestive system. Cats breathe faster and have faster heart rates than humans. They have powerful heads with strong muzzles for grasping prey, and 30 razor-sharp teeth to scissor through meat. There are no crushing teeth similar to human molars. The average domestic cat weighs about 5kg/9lb and stands about 30cm/12in high at the shoulder.

FELINE FACTS

• There are three basic cat shapes: cobby (solid build, short rounded head, short legs); muscular (medium build, medium legs, slightly rounded head); and lithe (light build, long slim legs, narrow wedge-shaped head).
• Cats cannot actually see in total darkness, but they do have extremely good vision even in very low light, being able to see about six times better than humans. Their pupils dilate widely to capture all available light, and at

the back of the eye is a mirror-like structure of cells called the tapetum lucidum which reflects light and causes the cat's eyes to 'glow' in the dark.

• Cats have about 120° of binocular vision and a further 80° of monocular vision. They do not see colour well, but this is not a handicap because perception of movement is more important.

• With eyesight, hearing is the cat's most important sense. Movable ears set high on the head channel sound to sensitive ear drums. Here, sound waves cause vibrations which travel as electrical impulses to the brain, where they are interpreted.

• Cats can hear extremely high- and low-frequency sounds, even up to 65 kHz, over three times higher than most humans.

Cats have extraordinary powers of co-ordination and balance. Contrary to myth, they do not always land unhurt if they fall, but they do tend to right themselves as they fall, and can land safely astonishingly often. A cat can manoeuvre on a narrow ledge using its tail for balance. Leathery paw pads and sharp claws help with grip and are good brakes. Cats walk on well-padded toes, and keep their claws retracted until they need to use them.

FELINE FACTS

• A cat's nose is filled with bony plates called turbinals which increase the surface area to accommodate more cells sensitive to smell.

• A cat has three times as many cells which are capable of detecting smell as humans.

• Cats have an unusual organ called Jacobson's organ in the roof of the mouth. This is sensitive to smells and tastes above those normally detected, and usually associated with sexual scents. Cats draw back their lips in a response called 'flehmen', a word which has no English translation. It describes the cat curling up its lips to draw a scent into its mouth and across the Jacobson's organ.

• A cat's tongue has horny projections called *filiform papillae* on it, which are useful not only for grooming but also for rasping meat off a bone, or for lapping up liquids. The tongue is extremely sensitive and can detect sweet, sour, salt and bitter, as well as temperature and texture.

• A cat's whiskers, 'vibrissae', are extremely sensitive, not just to touch but to atmospheric changes.

• Cats have scent glands on their chin and temples. They spread their scent by rubbing their heads and bodies against objects. Sweat glands on the foot pads also enable the cat to leave a scent when it scratches a post, branch or piece of furniture. Both sexes can also mark a territory by spraying urine.

Cat Reproduction and Life Cycle

A queen will come on heat, that is be ready to mate, several times a year. At such times she will call loudly, roll around extravagantly, and her urine will contain special chemicals called pheromones. These chemicals produce an odour attractive to tom cats and are capable of drifting long distances. When a tom cat arrives to mate with a queen, she will usually reject him at first. She will then adopt a mating position, with her tail to one side and her rear end in the air. The male grips her by the scruff of the neck. Mating is very brief, and may be repeated several times over a few days. Thus it is possible for a litter to contain kittens by more than one father.

FELINE FACTS

- The period of gestation is about 65 days.
- The average size of a litter is four kittens.
- The newborn kitten is about 10-15cm/4-6in long and weighs between 57-142g/2-5oz.
- Cats have eight teats, but can rear up to 14 kittens.
- The mother licks her kittens frequently. Licking stimulates breathing and circulation, and encourages regular defecation and urination.

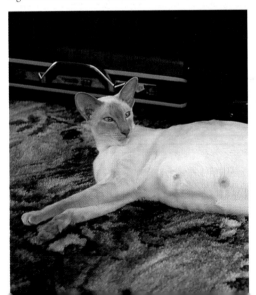

Kittens are usually crawling at two weeks old. They start to eat solid food at about three to four weeks old, and are totally weaned at eight weeks. Litter training can start at about 3 weeks and, as cats are naturally extremely fastidious animals, house training is not usually difficult to accomplish. At four weeks kittens are running, playing, and washing themselves. They are completely independent at three months.

FELINE FACTS

- Kittens' eyes are usually shut for the first week or so after birth. Smell and touch are their most important senses at this stage.
- At birth, all kittens have blue eyes, and both eye and coat colour, as well as coat pattern may change as they mature.
- At five weeks pedigree kittens should be registered with the relevant breed association.
- Permanent teeth start to come through at about twelve weeks.
- Toms should be neutered at between six and nine months. Females should be spayed at about the same age.

During the four or five months that kittens can spend with their mother before the maternal bonds have completely loosened, she will teach them everything they need to know to survive. She will even show them how to wash. Kittens who are taken early from their mother and are not taught to catch, kill and eat mice or other prey often never learn this skill. Really efficient mousers learn the art from a mother who is a good mouser herself.

FELINE FACTS

• Kittens should be handled – gently! – as much as possible to accustom them to living among humans and to encourage them to enjoy being stroked and lifted.

• When a cat is 10 years old, it is approximately equivalent in age to a human of 60 years old.

Cats live, on average, for between 9 and 15 years, though cats of 20 years and older are not uncommon. They are longer-lived than dogs, which is unusual as larger animals usually live longer than smaller ones. Neutered toms usually live longer than entire toms. 'Old age' in a cat is generally reckoned to be from about 10 to 12 years old, although many show no signs of ageing until 15 or 16 years.

FELINE FACTS

• Cats usually retain a good appetite well into old age and do not seem to suffer from aches and pains in the same way as old dogs.

• An older cat may have difficulty leaping as it is less supple.

- If it has trouble grooming itself, it may need some help.
- Like humans in old age, older cats usually prefer a well-established routine in life.
- They should be kept warm, and maybe given softer food if their teeth begin to be less than sound.

❧ CATS IN ACTION ❧

Hunting and Feeding

Cats are carnivores, with a gut adapted to eat meat. They cannot be vegetarians. They are natural hunters and even the best-fed house cat can be extremely skilful at catching small rodents or birds. However, only the rudiments of the hunting skill are instinctive, and the technique must be refined by lessons early in life. The mother cat will usually bring prey home to her litter to practise on, and even later in life playing with your cat will help it to hone its skills.

FELINE FACTS
• Cats hunt alone, and are models of stealth and patience. When prey is sighted, the cat presses its body

close to the ground and creeps forward, using every available bit of cover. Its pupils dilate and its ears prick forward, showing total concentration.

• When it is ready to pounce, it wiggles its hind quarters as if finding perfect balance for the take-off.

• The cat will trap its prey with both front feet and will often appear to play with it, throwing it in the air or letting it go, only to pounce on it again.

• The cat has three main patterns of attack:

When catching mice, it will bite down on the neck for the kill.

If a bird escapes and flies up, the cat will reach up with both front feet to trap it again.

Many cats are expert fishers, and use a 'dip and flip' technique. One paw scoops the fish out of the water and flips it over the cat's shoulder, when it can be trapped with the front paws.

• Many cats instinctively bring home their prey as trophies, and will not understand being scolded or punished.

Body Language

Cats communicate with their fellow cats and with humans in several ways. They vocalize, uttering a wide variety of complex sounds conveying warning, concern, excitement, pain, sexuality, discontent and many other emotions. Cats also express themselves by their posture and facial expressions. In addition, they communicate by touch and by smell.

FELINE FACTS

• It is thought that cats can make up to 17 different sounds in three main groups: they meow, hiss, and purr.

• It is not known for sure how the purr is created, but it is probably caused by the vibration of membranes located near the vocal cords.

• Some cats 'talk' more than others: Siamese cats are famously vocal.

• Cats make a tooth-chattering sound when in sight of prey but unable to reach it.

• A cat sitting with its feet tucked up under it and its eyes half closed is contented and comfortable.

• A cat crouching with its tail lashing low, its ears back, its mouth open and its pupils narrowed is angry and ready for a fight.

• A cat on the defensive will stand sideways to its aggressor with its tail and body fur fluffed up, its ears flat and its pupils dilated, or it will cringe down with its fur and whiskers flattened.

Nocturnal Activity

Cats are predominantly nocturnal, and prefer to hunt at night when their natural stealth helps to keep them hidden, and when their good night vision offers them an advantage. Their sensitive whiskers are also invaluable. The whiskers are responsive feelers, and are also efficient detectors of air currents, allowing the cat to manoeuvre safely in the dark without bumping into things. If a cat has damaged whiskers it may be able to kill cleanly in daylight, but it will not be able to do so in the dark.

FELINE FACTS

• Cats sleep for between 16 and 18 hours each day, during which time their senses remain alert and their brain active.

• Cats have a number of reinforced hairs similar to whiskers on other parts of their bodies: over the eyes, on the chin, and at the back of the legs.

• Cats' eyes contract to slits rather than circular pinpricks because it is important for an animal with such good vision not to be dazzled by bright light. With the pupils contracting to slits and with the eyelids closing horizontally, the cat can make an extremely delicate adjustment to the amount of light entering its eye.

Working Cats

The original decision by mankind to keep cats about them was almost certainly made because of the cat's proven abilities in pest control. In Ancient Egypt, cats probably started out protecting grain stores from rats, and later were regarded as sacred, with death the punishment for killing a cat. The Romans took cats with them as they conquered Europe, and the new domestic animal settled in everywhere as a valuable addition to the workforce.

FELINE FACTS

• The farm cat has the longest history of working cats. For a long time it was thought it was better to keep a working cat hungry, but actually a well-fed cat will have better stamina and reactions, and he will probably prefer to stay close to home. In cats, the urge to hunt is not totally linked to the urge to eat.

- Cats were vital crew members on board ships, and their kind fanned out into the world with British colonists, arriving in North America in the 16th century and in Australia in the 18th century.
- The world's champion ratter may be a tabby who lived at the old White City Stadium. In six years nearly 12,500 rats were caught – a rate of five or six a day.
- Cats have been on the payroll of the British Civil Service for most of this century. Before the Second World War, Rufus lived at the Treasury, drawing pay of tuppence a day. The then Chancellor of the Exchequer, Philip Snowden, increased his pay with a formal note: 'Treasury vote: approve increase of cat's pay.'
- English post office cats are granted an official subsistence allowance.

The value of a good mouser was recognized by Hywel the Good, Prince of South Wales, who in AD 936 enacted a law setting out the value of a cat: a kitten was worth a penny until it opened its eyes, then twopence until it caught its first mouse, when it was worth fourpence. If a cat guarding the royal corn was killed, wheat was required in compensation sufficient to cover the body of the cat completely when held up by its tail. Even today, cats are valued staff members at railway stations, riding stables, dockyards, museums and factories.

FELINE FACTS

• The National Printing Office of France keeps a staff of cats to protect the paper from mice.

- On patrol since 1988 in Jackson, Michigan, a cat called Feedback has put a stop to mice dining on the building's wiring.
- A police station in Texas is home to Fang, a cat who has his own photocard ID.
- When the Port of London was a working dockyard, it employed 100 cats to protect the valuable cargoes.
- Covent Garden Fruit and Vegetable Market relies on its cats to keep down the rodent population.
- Cats work in television too: in Japan a troop of cats has been trained to wear clothes and create tableaux, appearing in advertisements, on posters and on calendars.

NON-PEDIGREE
~ CATS ~

Introduction

Non-pedigree cats, 'moggies', are the most common kind of cat in the world. With their cobby bodies, round faces and soft fur, they are also some of the most appealing, and are to be found as much-loved family pets in many, many homes. With the principle of hybrid vigour, they are usually hardy and robust with few health problems, and can live to a great age. There are more tabbies than any other colour as tabby genes are dominant throughout the cat species, but many are bi-coloured. Eye colour and coat colour depend on nothing more scientific than chance. Left to nature it is rarely possible to breed a specific characteristic, as the father is seldom known, leaving only natural selection to provide longer coats for cats in colder climates.

These moggy cats, resilient and resourceful, spread throughout Europe with the Romans, usefully patrolling grain stores, stables and private houses against rodents. Wherever humans went, cats went with them: on ships, with armies, as settlers in strange lands. Often they lived rough. Black cats even survived centuries of persecution, being burnt as witches' familiars and being walled up alive in buildings to bring luck.

FELINE FACTS

- The basic type of cat is shorthaired, with a thick rough coat not liable to tangling or requiring owner care.
- Scottish Wild cats are usually tabby, because a patterned coat provides excellent camouflage.
- Where a harsh environment favoured the genetic mutation for a longer coat, wild longhairs have fur which they can maintain without the need for grooming.
- All cats are capable of remarkable perceptions and amazing self-reliance, and the non-pedigree cat often seems to choose his owner rather than the other way round.

Shorthaired Non-Pedigree Cats

BREED BASICS
Colours: All. **Coat Length:** Short.
Type of Fur: Usually thick and soft.
Markings: Any, but white patches are common.
Size: Any. **Characteristics:** Short, stocky body is usual,
with rounded face and short ears, often tufted.
Eyes tend to be round, usually greenish in colour.
Legs are usually stocky with round paws.
Tail is usually thick and soft.

Non-pedigree shorthairs are to be found in every imaginable combination of colour and pattern, though the most common type is the tabby, and foreign colours such as chocolate or lilac are comparatively rare.

By definition there is no standard type, but the short-haired non-pedigree does tend to be a cobby, stocky cat with a round face.

FELINE FACTS

• The white hairs which are such a feature of the non-pedigree have been bred out in the pedigree solid colours, where they are often regarded as a serious fault.
• The tortoiseshell colouration is the result of a red gene. This gene is sex linked, and tortoiseshell cats are nearly always female, with any males born tending to be sterile.

The natural range of the African Wild Cat, from which our domesticated cats originated, extends throughout not only Africa, but also the Middle East and the shores of the Mediterranean. The tabby pattern of this cat was not as definite as the modern tabby markings.

FELINE FACTS

• The striped, or mackerel, tabby has a coat of thin, dark lines, some broken, similar to the tiger's patterning.

• The blotched tabby was a mutation that originally arose in Elizabethan England. The markings are more complex and darker. The blotched tabby is the most common marking in the world.

• Old English saying: 'Honest as the cat when the meat's out of reach.'

Longhaired Non-Pedigree Cats

BREED BASICS
Colours: Any. **Coat Length:** Long.
Type of Fur: Thick and soft. **Markings:** Any.
Size: Any. **Characteristics:** Usually a stocky, strong body, a more-or-less rounded head and an alert expression. Fur is often deeply ruffed round the neck and as knickerbockers. Eyes are usually greenish in colour. Paws are usually untufted. Even solid colours often show traces of tabby marking.

Many of today's long-haired pedigree cats have domestic non-pedigree cousins, living comfortable lives on farms or as house pets with families. The Angora still walks the streets of the hilltop village of Angora in Turkey, his looks rather different from the cats exhibited as Angoras at cat shows.

FELINE FACTS
• Cat shows often have a class for non-pedigree animals, where judgement is based on overall looks and condition.
• Some believe that tortoiseshell cats have a reputation for being good mothers. But it is a tabby cat from Texas in the USA who has given birth to 420 kittens during her lifetime.

According to pet food manufacturers, there are more than 7 million domestic cats in the UK, and about 57 million in the USA. Cat ownership is growing by leaps and bounds. City-dwellers, wanting company but with no facilities to keep a dog and little time for the exercise a dog demands, find a cat the ideal pet. Many who are out all day keep two cats to be company for each other. Pet owners are said to be healthier and to live longer than non-pet owners. Stroking an animal actually reduces blood pressure as well as relieving anxiety and loneliness.

FELINE FACTS

• Many non-pedigree longhairs are just as good-looking as pedigrees, and are often available free. They can be more robust, less fussy eaters and healthier.

• When choosing a non-pedigree cat, remember that a longhaired cat will require as much grooming and brushing as any pedigree animal.

• Parasites such as fleas can be difficult to spot on longhaired cats, so it is important to keep a good look-out when you are grooming your cat.

• If your longhaired cat gets very wet in the rain, make sure you dry her thoroughly, and if possible keep her in a warm room until the last traces of dampness have disappeared.

• Most cat shows have a class for non-pedigree animals, and the longhair section can be a difficult one to judge, as longhaired cats are usually exceptionally graceful and attractive.

THE
~ PEDIGREE CAT ~

Recognized Breeds

The notion of a recognized breed of cat arose in Britain in the 19th century, leading to the first Cat Show, organized by Harrison Weir in 1871 at the Crystal Palace in London. It was followed not long afterwards by the first cat show in North America. At that time, the British cat shows had classes only for British Shorthairs and for Persians, but today there are about 100 recognized breeds of cat. Some are available worldwide, and some are recognized only in certain countries.

FELINE FACTS

There are eight different categories of recognized breed, if you count the domestic non-pedigree cat.

- Longhairs of Persian type: these conform to the same ideal type.
- Longhairs of non-Persian type: for example the Maine Coon. The only factor these have in common is long hair.
- British and American Shorthairs.
- Other Shorthairs, not fitting into any other Shorthair group: for example the Abyssinian, the Egyptian Mau, the Rex.
- Oriental Shorthairs: usually Siamese in shape and size but not displaying the restricted coat pattern of the Siamese (genetically called the Himalayan factor).
- Burmese.
- Siamese.

In Britain, classification is decided by the Governing Council of the Cat Fancy (GCCF) and by the Cat Association. In the USA there are several organizations, including the oldest, the American Cat Association, and

the largest, the Cat Fanciers' Association. Each country's cat associations establish standards for breeds, provide for registration of kittens and transfer of ownership, and also approve show dates.

FELINE FACTS

- Even the most aristocratic of pedigree cats is usually a family pet, so it is important that whatever breed of cat is chosen should fit in with your life style.
- Do not buy a cat with a luxuriously long coat if you do not have the time to groom it, and remember that Siamese and Burmese cats can be very demanding of your company.
- Breeds vary in temperament and character as well as in looks.
- Standards set by cat associations are for ideal appearance – body shape, colouration and pattern. Recently, temperament has also been considered by show judges.

Cats from North America

The first all-American cat show for pedigree cats was held in 1895 in New York, and since then Americans have enthusiastically embraced the breeding of all kinds of cat, from the long-established Persians to newer, more unusual types of cat. In fact, most of the recently developed breeds of cat have originated in North America – usually in the United States, although the Sphynx was developed in Canada.

FELINE FACTS

• The Maine Coon is the first Longhair breed to originate in North America. Maine Coons were being shown at informal cat shows in America as long ago as the 1860s.

• The ancestors of the American Shorthairs probably reached North America with English settlers in the 16th century. With their hardy heritage, they are larger and stronger than their British cousins. They have been recognized as a breed since the early 1900s.

• One of the most important tasks of cat associations is to guard against the development of freakish breeds in which the characteristics of the cat may be detrimental to its health. For instance, the Munchkin, which is currently being developed in America, has very short legs which could make the breed vulnerable to arthritis.

Unusual Cats

New and unusual breeds of cat are often developed from a chance mutation, in the quest for the novel and different. Once such kittens would probably have been put down, but today commercial opportunities are often spotted. Mutations are not always harmful, but they are occasionally developed at a cost to the cat. One of nature's most independent and self-reliant creatures can end up totally dependent on humans. Hairless Sphynxes, for example, could not survive outside the home; the stunted Munchkin may not be able to fend for itself.

FELINE FACTS

• The Scottish Fold and the American Curl are two breeds in which a chance mutation which caused deformed ears has been established. Breeders are adamant that the unusual shape of the ears causes the cats no discomfort.

• It is harder to obtain recognition for such cats from the GCCF in Great Britain than from the cat associations of the United States.

There are a number of older breeds of unusual cat. The Rex type (the Cornish, the Devon and the Selkirk) dates from the 1950s: earlier specimens having the short, crimped coat were destroyed as freaks. The Manx cat has been known on the Isle of Man, off the west coast of England, for centuries. Perhaps if it were to have been developed today we might find more fault with the idea of a cat with no tail.

FELINE FACTS

• The Turkish Van is unusual in that it seems to like swimming. Of the big cats, only tigers are strong swimmers, and domestic cats usually shy away from water in any form.

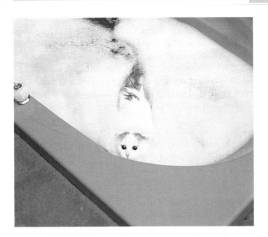

Cat Shows

The first formal show for pedigree cats was organized by Harrison Weir in 1871 at Crystal Palace in London. There were 160 exhibits at the show, all of which were judged according to specific standards, now known as the 'standard of points'. These have changed over the years, sometimes greatly, but the basic arrangement of cat shows has remained constant. Today cat associations all over the world establish standards of points and put on cat shows. In the case of some breeds, the standards are common all over the world; in others, the standards vary from country to country.

FELINE FACTS

- In the UK, most shows are run under the rules of the Governing Council of the Cat Fancy (GCCF).
- Some shows are for all breeds, and some are for one breed only. Shows vary from small local affairs to major national ones, such as the National Cat Club Show, held in London and probably the largest championship in the world.
- There are three types of show in Britain: the Exemption, the Sanction; and the Championship.
- Championship shows are major events. Winners may be awarded certificates which count towards the title of Champion.
- The Exemption is usually small and not very formal; at the Sanction no Challenge or Premier certificates are awarded, so winning does not count towards the title of Champion.

At cat shows there are various categories and classes. There is usually an Open category, which is the most important. All pedigree cats are eligible to enter the Open, and there are classes for entire adults, neutered adults, kittens, with males and females in each class. There is often an Assessment category for new breeds which have only preliminary recognition from the GCCF. Then there may be an Exhibition category for non-competing cats. In this category may be new colours, or breeds which have yet to be recognized. In Britain these are the only pens which may be decorated and in which the cats may be identified. Lastly, there may be categories for non-pedigree cats, categories sponsored by specific cat clubs, and Side Classes (for example for cats who have never been shown before).

FELINE FACTS

• Winners of Open classes receive Challenge certificates. Holders of three Challenge certificates are eligible to be called Champions, and may enter a Champion of Champions class. A three-times winner of this may be called a Grand Champion.

• Neutered cats follow the same procedure, but receive Premier certificates, and become Premier Champions.

• Faults in any breed include: kinks in the tail, extra toes, missing testicles, an uneven jawline, a misaligned bite and white hairs except where white is part of the coat colour.

• Declawed cats are not eligible to enter a show

Shows take place throughout the year, and are advertised in specialist magazines. The sponsoring organization will be able to provide an entry form and a copy of the show rules. The rules often specify a compulsory week's gap between entering a cat in shows. Another common restraint is on anything which might alter the cat's appearance. A cat must hold current certificates of vaccination, be in good health and may not be pregnant.

FELINE FACTS

• A cat should be transported to the show in a sturdy basket or cage. Accustom your cat to car travel – motion sickness can look like a more serious ailment and could cause your cat to be disqualified.

• Your cat will require a water dish, clean litter tray and a clean white blanket for shows in the UK.

• In Britain, a vet is always in attendance at a major cat show, and the first procedure is 'vetting in', when the cat is examined for general health and for parasites of all kinds.

• The cat is then placed in its pen, a metal cage displaying its show entry number. You should make sure your cat is accustomed to being penned. Give it plenty of time to settle in before judging starts.

• Judging is against an accepted standard of points for pedigree cats, 100 points in all to be awarded. For non-pedigree cats, judges will look at condition, grooming, temperament and any special features.

• Rosettes are given to winners.

SHORTHAIRED
☙ BREEDS ❧

Introduction

Short fur is normal for wild cats, and most domestic cats have short fur. Longer fur occurs in the wild only where extreme cold demands it, such as in Siberia, where the Siberian Tiger lives in temperatures well below freezing. Short fur is easier to keep clean, and pest- and tangle-free, both for the cat itself and for its owner. Short fur is also genetically dominant, and so there will always be short-haired cats.

There are many different types of shorthair coat, from the soft, fine fur of the Rex, to the sleek Siamese, to the dense coat of the Manx.

There are three main categories of shorthaired cats: British, American, and Foreign (or Oriental). The British type is cobby and strong with short legs and a short, dense coat. It has a broad, round head and rounded eyes. There is no difference between this type and the European Shorthair.

The American Shorthair is a larger and more athletic cat with longer legs. The head is more oblong than round.

The Foreign Shorthair looks completely different from either of the two above. Its body is slender and lissome with long slim legs, and it has a wedge-shaped head with slanting eyes and long, pointed ears. Its coat is much shorter and finer than the British or American Shorthairs. The Siamese is a good example of the type.

Egyptian Mau

BREED BASICS

Colours: Silver, Black, Smoke, Pewter and Bronze.
Coat Length: Short. **Type of Fur:** Soft and dense.
Markings: Round spots all over the body, dark stripe
down the back changing to bands on the tail and legs.
'M' shaped mark on centre of forehead.
Dark lines running across cheeks.
Size: Medium. Female slightly smaller than male.
Characteristics: Unusually large green eyes in rounded
face. Eye colour changes as the cat matures, from dark
to pale. Large pointed ears. Brown or black paw pads.
Body markings also develop with maturity.

In the 1950s, Princess Natalia Troubetskoye, a member
of one of Russia's oldest families, mated a silver
spotted female from Cairo in Egypt with her smoke
spotted Egyptian tom, and the resulting bronze spotted
kittens, born in Italy where the princess was living, she
called Egyptian Maus. The breed was only officially
recognized in the USA in 1968 and in the UK in 1978,
yet these cats are the direct descendants of the very first
domestic cats living in Ancient Egypt.

FURTHER INFORMATION
• The name Mau comes from the Egyptian word for cat.
• In the UK, the breed is sometimes called the Oriental
Spotted Tabby.

• The Ancient Egyptians believed that cats' eyes are reflective at night because they contained the rays of the sun.

Sphynx

BREED BASICS
Colours: A wide range of colours.
Coat Length: Hairless, covering of soft down.
Type of Fur: No fur. Skin soft and suede-like.
Markings: Skin pigment gives colour to body.
Size: Medium, slender build.
Characteristics: Eye colour should match coat colour.
The ears are very large and have rounded tips. The
skin is wrinkled on parts of the body and head. There
may be soft down at the body extremities.

A hairless kitten born in Ontario, Canada, in the
1960s was used to develop this breed. There is some
evidence that the Aztec Indians encouraged naked cats
in their domestic breeds, and the Mexican Hairless was
popular for a short time in the 1880s. Not everyone will
find these delicate animals appealing, but they are
affectionate by nature and their skins are warm and soft
with a silky feel. Their lack of hair renders them more
vulnerable than most cats, so they are heavily reliant on
humans for protection. The breed is rare outside the
USA.

FURTHER INFORMATION
• As they have no fur, Sphynxes should be protected
from strong sunlight and from cold or draughts. They
are apt to shiver.

• Sphynxes are said to eat frequently to maintain their relatively high body temperature because they do not store body fat.

'Cats are a mysterious kind of folk. There is more passing in their minds than we are aware of.' – Sir Walter Scott (1771-1832).

Snowshoe

BREED BASICS

Colours: Seal-point, blue-point.
Coat Length: Short. **Type of Fur:** Rich and thick.
Markings: White feet and Siamese-like colourpoints.
Size: Medium to large, with males much larger than females. **Characteristics:** Tranquil personality, face more rounded than Siamese, medium size legs and paws. Pink and grey paw pads. Blue eyes. Large pointed ears, long tapering tail.

Snowshoes were developed in the United States in the 1960s by Dorothy Hinds-Daugherty, a breeder of Siamese cats who used American Bicoloured Shorthairs to establish the new breed. At first other breeders were suspicious of the new cat, fearing the dilution of the pedigree Siamese line, but nowadays these pretty cats with their delicate white feet are popular in several countries of the world. The Snowshoe was recognized for championship status in the USA in 1983.

FURTHER INFORMATION

• Kittens are born white and it may take up to two years for markings to develop. As the cat ages, the colouration darkens.

• Colour is also darker in colder climates.

• The Snowshoe is sometimes called the Silver Lace because the white paws slightly resemble those of the Birman.

In Ancient Rome the cat was a symbol of liberty and the goddess of liberty was represented with a cat at her feet.

Abyssinian

BREED BASICS

Varieties: Usual (Ruddy brown with black or dark brown ticking), Sorrel (Copper-red with chocolate ticking), Blue (blue-grey with steel blue ticking), Fawn (Medium fawn with deep fawn ticking), Lilac (pinkish grey with darker pinkish-grey ticking), Silver (silver with black ticking), Silver Sorrel (silvery peach with chocolate ticking), Silver Blue (silvery blue-grey with deep steel-blue ticking). **Coat Length:** Short.
Type of Fur: Dense and glossy. **Markings:** Ticked fur colour, caused by at least four bands of light and dark colour on each shaft of hair. **Size:** Medium.
Characteristics: Muscular body with long legs and small oval feet. Wedge-shaped head with large, wide-set ears following the shape of the wedge. Eyes almond shaped and amber, hazel or green in colour, rimmed with dark brown or black and with an outer, paler circle. Tapering, thickly-furred tail.

These ancient, mysterious-looking cats may be one of the oldest breeds of domestic cat. Abyssinian cats were first brought to Britain by soldiers returning from war in Abyssinia (now called Ethiopia) in 1868. They make good pets, being gentle and intelligent; indeed some claim they may easily be trained. They have a very distinctive voice which has been described as 'bell-like'.

FURTHER INFORMATION

• It is said that more Abyssinian males are born than females and, although they mature early, coat markings may not develop for nearly two years.

• Abyssinians tend to have small litters, and thus they are one of the world's most expensive breeds of cat.

• At one time, the Usual variety was known as the Rabbit Cat for the similarity of its coat to that of a rabbit.

Witches are said to have a black cat as their familiar, or spirit slave. This superstition may have arisen from the classical legend of Galenthias, who was turned into a cat and became a priestess of Hecate, the Greek goddess of witchcraft.

American Shorthair

BREED BASICS

Coat Length: Short. **Type of Fur:** Thick and coarse.
Markings: Many coat patterns. **Size:** Larger than their
British counterparts. **Characteristics:** Strong, powerful
body with dense fur to suit an outdoor life and
muscular jaws to kill prey. Robust health and
well-developed curiosity as befits good hunters. Head
large and rounded, with rounded eyes and pink nose
pad. Large paws, with pads matching coat colour.

European cats taken to North America during the
16th century are the ancestors of these hardy, robust
cats. Originally valued for their hunting skills and
strength they flourished, despite the arduous conditions
in the early Spanish settlements in southern North
America as well as in the British and French settlements
further north. They have been recognized as a breed
since the early years of the 20th century.

FURTHER INFORMATION

• American Shorthairs are robust and active and need
to spend plenty of time out of doors.
• The original settlers in North America took cats with
them specifically to kill rats and mice, first on the ships
in which they sailed and then in their new homes.

During the Second World War, Britain received
indispensable help from the local population in

Burma only because an English colonel, familiar with the beliefs of the people and the folklore of the country, had white cats painted on all vehicles and road plans.

VARIETIES AND COLOURS OF AMERICAN SHORTHAIR

White (pure white), Black (pure black), Blue (pale blue-grey), Red (dark red), Cream (buff), Bicolour (white with black, red, blue or cream patches), Shaded Silver (white undercoat with mantle of black tips), Chinchilla Silver (pure white undercoat with black tips), Shell Cameo (white undercoat with red tips), Shaded Cameo (white undercoat with longer red tips than Shell Cameo), Red Smoke (white undercoat with deep red tipping), Black Smoke (white undercoat with black tips), Blue Smoke (white undercoat with deep blue tips), Blue-cream (blue with cream patches), Tortoiseshell (black with red and cream patches), Tortoiseshell Smoke (white undercoat with black, red and cream tips in tortie pattern), Van Pattern (white with auburn patches), Calico (white with black and red patches), Dilute Calico (white with blue and cream patches), Brown Tabby (brown with black classic or mackerel markings), Red Tabby (red with red classic or mackerel markings), Silver Tabby (silver with black classic or mackerel markings), Blue Tabby (pale blue with deep blue classic or mackerel markings), Cream Tabby (pale cream with buff classic or mackerel markings), Cameo Tabby (off-white with red classic or mackerel markings), Patched Tabby (silver, brown or blue with black, dark grey or red/cream patches in classic or mackerel pattern).

American Wirehair

BREED BASICS

Varieties: Tortie and White, Brown Mackerel Tabby,
Tortie and White Van. **Colours:** Available in all the
same colours as the American Shorthair.
Coat Length: Short. **Type of Fur:** Crimped and dense,
similar to a lamb's fleece. Fur requires several days to
regain its curl after getting wet.
Markings: Available in all the same coat markings as
for the American Shorthair. **Size:** Medium to large.
Characteristics: Frizzy coat somewhat similar to lamb's
wool, with crimped whiskers. Rounded head and eyes,
medium legs and tail. Eye colouration should
correspond to coat colour. Long-lived and healthy,
with lively temperament.

These rare cats, almost unknown outside North
America, were bred from a wiry-haired kitten born
in New York State in 1967. Wirehaired feral cats have
been reported in other countries, notably in Britain after
the Second World War, but they never became established.
American Wirehairs were given championship status in
the USA by the CFA in 1977.

Wirehairs have affectionate natures and make
excellent pets. The kittens are born with tightly-curled,
woolly coats, and it takes up to six months for the coat
to relax into adult texture.

FURTHER INFORMATION

• The wirehaired characteristic is dominant, and provided one parent is wirehaired the litter will contain wirehaired kittens.

According to Carl Van Vechten, Champfleury counted 63 different notes in the mewing of a cat, although, he admitted, it took an accurate ear to hear them all.

Bombay

BREED BASICS

Varieties: None. **Colours:** Black.
Coat Length: Short. **Type of Fur:** Thick and
gleaming, like patent leather. **Markings:** None. The
fur is a single colour from root to tip. **Size:** Medium.
Characteristics: Wedge-shaped face with eyes gold or
yellow. Nose leather, paw pads and eye rims solid
black or very dark brown. Medium to large ears with
rounded tips and slight forward tilt. Medium to long
straight tail, carried proud. Strong, muscular body
with straight back. Medium legs with oval paw pads.

Nikki Horner of Kentucky bred the first of these black panther look-alikes in 1958, from a Sable Burmese and a Black American Shorthair. The breed is named for the city of Bombay where black panthers are to be found. Bombays make ideal family pets, as they are highly affectionate and adore human company. They can be perfectly content to spend most of their life indoors. They are strikingly good-looking with their glossy black coats and golden eyes.

FURTHER INFORMATION

- Bombay kittens have tabby markings at birth. Their eyes, blue at birth like all kittens, change to grey before becoming the characteristic adult copper colour.
- The black panther is actually just a genetic mutation of the leopard, living in the forest where black colouration or spots provide good camouflage.

British Self Shorthair

BREED BASICS

Colours: White, Cream, Blue, Blue-Cream, Chocolate, Lilac, Red. **Coat Length:** Short.
Type of Fur: Dense and springy.
Markings: No markings should be present.
Size: Medium, stocky body.
Characteristics: Rounded face and cobby body, with strong broad shoulders and short legs. Ears are small with rounded tips and set well apart. Nose is short and straight with pad appropriately coloured to match coat. Eyes copper, orange or deep gold (except for the blue-eyed and odd-eyed White) and well-rounded.

Until the turn of the century, the British Shorthair was the most popular cat at the newly-established shows at Crystal Palace in London. Then the exotic Persian and Siamese breeds started to become fashionable, but the Shorthair has never lost its place in the hearts of the nation.

FURTHER INFORMATION

• The White variety, like all white cats, is at risk from sunburn. Whites can sometimes have one orange eye and one blue eye. They can suffer from deafness.

Cats have an extraordinary ability to land safely. In under two seconds they are able to rotate their body from upside down to a right-side-up landing stance with all four paws ready.

British Black Shorthair

BREED BASICS
Colours: Black. **Coat Length:** Short.
Type of Fur: Dense and springy. **Size:** Medium,
stocky body. **Characteristics:** Rounded face and cobby
body, with strong broad shoulders and short legs. Paw
pads black. Ears are small and set well apart. Nose is
short and straight with black nose leather. Eyes
copper-coloured and well rounded.

Pedigree British Shorthairs were
evolved in the 1880s from
the best of ordinary domestic
cats, and are now often
crossed with Persians to
give a more rounded
head. Since the 1930s
new colours have also
been developed.
These cats are
placid, good-
natured animals
and with their
intelligence and
hunting skills make
excellent house cats
and mousers. European
Shorthair breeds are identical.

FURTHER INFORMATION

• Black cats have over the years, and even to this day, been regarded by some as bringers of bad luck and by others as creatures of good omen.

 Siamese cats are prone to being born with extra toes. One Siamese was born with 26 toes instead of the normal 18.

British Tabby Shorthair

> **BREED BASICS**
> **Colours:** Silver, brown, red, cream, blue.
> **Coat Length:** Short. **Type of Fur:** Dense and springy.
> **Markings:** Classic, mackerel, and spotted (or
> blotched), with 'M' on forehead. Complete rings on
> tail, even barring on legs. **Size:** Medium, stocky body.
> **Characteristics:** Rounded face and cobby body, with
> strong broad shoulders and short legs. Ears are small
> and set well apart. The eyes are most usually
> copper-coloured and well rounded (except Silver
> Tabby which has green or hazel eyes). Nose is short
> and straight, coloured to match coat.

Today's British Shorthairs are descended from cats brought to Britain by Caesar's soldiers. Careful breeding since the 19th century has produced cats of set standards.

FURTHER INFORMATION

• It is said that the prophet Mohammed once embraced a tabby cat. He left his initial on its forehead, and to this day all tabby cats have a characteristic 'M' shaped marking on their forehead.

• The word 'tabby' is said to come from Attabiya, an area of old Baghdad where a striped cloth known as tabbi silk was woven.

British Spotted Shorthair

The coat of the British Spotted Shorthair is very similar to a mackerel tabby's, with the stripes broken into spots. These are strikingly beautiful cats, especially in the silver colouring.

FURTHER INFORMATION

• In Ancient Egyptian mythology, the sun god Ra in the form of a spotted cat severed the head of the serpent Apop, god of darkness and chaos.

London's most superior cat may have been Jackson, the mascot at the Embassy Club in Bond Street. His trick was to jump through a waiter's circled arms, and he liked to be rewarded with titbits of foie gras, smoked salmon or roast quail. Jackson died young, perhaps because of his rich diet.

British Tortoiseshell Shorthair

BREED BASICS

Varieties: Tortoiseshell, Blue-cream, Chocolate Tortie, Lilac Tortie. **Colours:** Base colour patched with red and cream. **Coat Length:** Short. **Type of Fur:** Dense and springy. **Markings:** Patches in various patterns, colours clearly defined. **Size:** Medium, stocky body. **Characteristics:** Rounded face and cobby body, with strong broad shoulders and short legs. Ears are small and set well apart. Nose is short and straight. Eyes well rounded and copper or orange in colour. Nose leather and paw pads should correspond with coat colour.

Tortoiseshell cats are by no means rare, but they are surprisingly difficult to breed in this pattern. Even in the most favourable circumstances a litter may only contain one tortie kitten. In the USA, tortoiseshell and white cats are called calico.

FURTHER INFORMATION

• Because sex and colour are genetically linked, tortoiseshell cats are nearly always female. The rare male tortoiseshell will be infertile.

'A home without a cat, and a well-fed, well-petted and properly revered cat, may be a

perfect home, *perhaps*, but how can it prove its title?'
– Mark Twain.

British Bi-colour Shorthair

BREED BASICS

Colours: Black, Cream, Red, Blue, Chocolate, Lilac.
Coat Length: Short. **Type of Fur:** Dense and springy.
Markings: Clear, even patches of one self colour with white. **Size:** Medium, stocky body.
Characteristics: Rounded face and cobby body, with strong broad shoulders and short legs. Ears are small and set well apart. Nose is short and straight. Nose leather should be pink or correspond with coat colour. Eyes well rounded and should be copper or orange in colour with no green on the rims. Colour should be present on the face.

Bi-coloured cats, with their white coats patched with another colour, are a common sight in every neighbourhood, but the pedigree version sets a difficult standard to attain. The original standard required the patching to be symmetrical, but it is rarely possible to achieve this, and now all that is demanded is that the patches should be clear and even, with up to two-thirds coloured and the white between one-third and one-half.

FURTHER INFORMATION

• This breed was only recognized for showing in 1966, having previously been displayed in the 'other variety' classes.

At Chelmsford, in England, a number of Roman roof tiles have been found, bearing the clear imprint of a cat's paws. It must have been difficult to keep the local moggies out of the tile-drying yard!

British Smoke Shorthair

BREED BASICS

Colours: Blue, Black, Chocolate, Lilac, Red, Cream, Tortie, Blue Tortie, Chocolate Tortie, Lilac Tortie.

Coat Length: Short. **Type of Fur:** Dense and springy.

Markings: Silver undercoat with self or tortie colour topcoat. No tabby markings should appear.

Size: Medium, stocky body.

Characteristics: Rounded face and cobby body, with strong broad shoulders and short legs.

Ears are small and set well apart. Nose is short and straight. Nose leather and paw pads correspond to coat colour. Eyes well rounded and should be copper or orange in colour.

This breed was developed in the late 19th century by crossing Silver Tabby and solid British Shorthairs. Smokes have a very unusual coat. They have a single-colour topcoat of either black or blue over a white undercoat. When the cat moves, the white flickers through, creating a unique shimmering effect.

FURTHER INFORMATION

• Two distinct genes are responsible for the smoke coat of these cats. One inhibits colouration in the undercoat, and the other emphasizes colour along the guard hairs.

It's not uncommon to hear of a cat being remembered in its owner's will. In 1988, a wealthy

Englishwoman, Mrs Walker, left £3 million to an animal charity on condition that they looked after her cat until he died.

British Tipped Shorthair

BREED BASICS

Colours: Black, Blue, Chocolate, Lilac, Red, Cream, Black Tortie, Blue Tortie, Chocolate Tortie, Lilac Tortie, Golden. **Coat Length:** Short. **Type of Fur:** Dense and springy. **Markings:** Pale undercoat with coloured tipping. No tabby markings should be present except some vestigial tail rings. The chin, chest and stomach should be white. **Size:** Medium, stocky body. **Characteristics:** Rounded face and cobby body, with strong broad shoulders and short legs. Paw pads appropriately coloured to match coat. Ears are small and set well apart. Nose is short and straight with brick-red pad outlined in colour appropriate to colour of coat tipping. Eyes well rounded and should be copper or orange in colour rimmed in colour appropriate to the colour of the tipping, or green with black rims in the black variety.

The British Tipped Shorthair was once known as the Chinchilla Shorthair, and this breed has only been known under its new name since 1978. They are the result of an intricate breeding programme involving Blues, Silvers and Smokes.

FURTHER INFORMATION

• The kittens of many breeds take months before their adult markings develop. In tipped kittens, it is possible to see their Chinchilla Longhair ancestry quite clearly before they acquire their adult coats.

Himmy, an Australian cat, was so fat that, at 46lb, he found walking arduous and had to be wheeled round in a wheelbarrow.

British Colourpoint Shorthair

BREED BASICS

Varieties: Self, Tortie, Tabby. **Colours:** Cream, Seal, Chocolate, Blue, Red, Lilac, Blue-cream.
Coat Length: Short. **Type of Fur:** Dense and springy.
Markings: Coloured points on face, paws, tail and ears with good colour contrast. **Size:** Medium, stocky body. **Characteristics:** Rounded face and cobby body, with strong broad shoulders and short legs. Ears are small and set well apart. Nose is short and straight with pad appropriate colour to match coat. Eyes blue and well rounded.

These cats have been developed very recently, with breed recognition in Great Britain only since 1991. They display Siamese-type colourpoints, while retaining Shorthair body type.

FURTHER INFORMATION

• There are only the slightest of differences between European Shorthairs and their cousins, British Shorthairs. Indeed, they have only been recognized as a separate breed since 1982. They are good quality house cats with quite ordinary origins, probably descended ultimately from the African Wild Cat and brought to northern Europe by the Romans 2000 years ago. Left alone to breed they are an extremely robust animal and make excellent mousers. They are apt to have larger litters than other breeds, and with fewer problems.

Minstrel was a cat employed by the police. His job was to walk up and down in front of a line of police dogs in training: the dogs' task was to learn to ignore a cat temptingly strolling by.

Burmese

BREED BASICS

Varieties/Colours: Brown, Champagne, Platinum in the USA: in the UK Cream, Red, Chocolate, Lilac, Blue, Brown, Chocolate Tortie, Lilac Tortie, Blue Tortie, Brown Tortie. **Coat Length:** Short.

Type of Fur: Sleek and satiny.

Markings: Widely varied, including tortoiseshell.

Size: Medium. **Characteristics:** Medium-sized, muscular body with round chest and straight back. Slender legs, hind legs slightly longer than forelegs, paws oval in shape. Triangular face with large eyes rounded on the lower line. Eye colour golden yellow to amber. Medium, wide-set ears with outer line continuing profile of face and rounded at tips. Tail straight, should reach to the shoulder.

Brown Burmese cats have lived in Burma for many centuries, but the modern breed was founded by Wong Mau, a Siamese cat taken to the USA in the 1930s. The breed was officially recognized by the CFA in 1936, reached Great Britain in 1948, and since then a wide range of colours has been developed. The American strain retains a stocky body shape, whereas in Britain a slim body is preferred. These are frisky, fairly demanding cats, and are not quite as talkative as their Siamese ancestors.

FURTHER INFORMATION

• Burmese cats can have very large litters: the record is 19 kittens in a single litter.

• It is quite possible to train a Burmese to retrieve, just like a dog.

Singapura

BREED BASICS

Varieties: None. **Colours:** Cream or ivory.
Coat Length: Short. **Type of Fur:** Sleek and satiny.
Markings: Bands of bronze, with dark seal brown
ticking. Underparts usually lighter in colour.
Size: This breed is the smallest in the world,
often weighing only around 2.7kg/6lb.
Characteristics: Eyes and nose are outlined in black.
Eyes are large and almond-shaped. Ears are large and
slightly pointed. Tail is fairly short with a blunt end
and is darker than the rest of the body. Paws have
brown pads.

This breed was developed in the USA by Tommy Meadow during the 1970s from the feral cats of Singapore (Singapura is the Malaysian name for Singapore). These feral cats led a streetwise, scrounging life in the city's sewers, and were known as 'Drain Cats'. The new breed is still rare even in the USA, and consequently these cats are extremely valuable. They are cautious, shy animals, but the females are excellent mothers.

FURTHER INFORMATION

• The official mascot of Singapore is a Singapura cat named Kucinta, and there is a statue of a Singapura cat on the Singapore river.

• Feral cats from South-East Asia have been the basis of other new breeds in recent years as well as the Singapura, for example the Wild Abyssinian.

Japanese Bobtail

BREED BASICS

Varieties: Black, Red and White, Tortoiseshell and White. **Colours:** Usually tortoiseshell but other colours do occur. **Coat Length:** Medium. **Type of Fur:** Soft and silky. **Markings:** Usually tortoiseshell but other patterns do occur. **Size:** Medium. **Characteristics:** Triangular head with long nose and oval eyes. Large pointed ears set well forward on the head. Legs are long and slim, with the hind legs appreciably longer than the forelegs.

This breed has been known and revered in Japan for many hundreds of years, and the breed made its way to the USA after the Second World War with returning soldiers. Prints and models of these 'maneki-neko', or 'beckoning cats', adorn many Japanese homes. Bobtails were only recognized by North American cat fancy organizations and by the CFA in Japan in 1968. The breed is still rare in Britain and Europe. The gene responsible for the deformed tail probably crossed to Japan from China about 1000 years ago, as cats with this characteristic are common in many parts of Asia.

The tail is usually about 10cm/4in long with fused joints. The fur here is longer than that on the body, creating a powder puff effect. These cats are extremely friendly and vocal.

FURTHER INFORMATION

• Japanese Bobtails are often depicted with one paw raised in greeting, and the gesture is believed to be lucky.

 The ship's cat on Captain Scott's expedition to the South Pole in 1912 had his own hammock on board. He was the first of his species to land and overwinter in Antarctica, but unhappily was swept overboard in a gale and perished.

Korat

BREED BASICS

Varieties: None. **Colours:** Dusky silver-blue.
Coat Length: Short. **Type of Fur:** Flat and silky,
lacking a full undercoat. **Markings:** None.
Size: Medium. **Characteristics:** Semi-cobby body with
back carried in a curve. Heart-shaped face, round
green eyes, large round-tipped ears with sparse
furnishings, small paws with dark blue or pinkish
lavender pads, five toes in front, four at back. Tail
medium with a round tip.

Korats, known for many centuries in their native
Thailand as Si-sawat (meaning 'lucky'), were
renamed for the Korat region of the country by King
Rama V in the 19th century . The first Korats reached
Britain at the same time as Siamese cats, at the end of
the 19th century, but were not recognized as a breed
until 1966 in the USA, and 1975 in Great Britain. They
are exceptionally good-natured and intelligent, but
because of their tropical origins they lack a full
undercoat, and they should be protected from cold
weather. Breeders are always careful to maintain the
traditional appearance of the Korat.

FURTHER INFORMATION

• In country areas, these stormy-coloured Korats are
believed to have power over the weather, and at the end

of a dry season, farmers would pour water over a cat to encourage rain.
• Korats are also thought to bring prosperity and good fortune, and are often given as wedding gifts.
• In the medieval Siamese Cat Book Poems, the Korat is described as having 'smooth hairs with tips like clouds and roots like silver, and eyes that shine like dewdrops on a lotus leaf'.

Havana

BREED BASICS

Varieties: Frost (exclusive to the USA).
Colours: Chestnut brown, Frost.
Coat Length: Very short. **Type of Fur:** Dense and
glossy, close-lying. **Markings:** None.
Size: Medium. **Characteristics:** Long, slender body
with long slim legs. Hind legs longer than forelegs.
Small oval paws with brown or pink pads. Head is
long and wedge-shaped and almond-shaped green
eyes. Nose leather brown or pinkish brown. Ears are
large and pointed. Tail long and tapering.

The Havana is the result of a cross between a
Seal-point Siamese and a black shorthaired cat, and
the breed was recognized in 1958. Havanas are judged
by a different standard in the USA from that used in
Britain. By prohibiting the use of Siamese cats in their
breeding programme, American breeders produced a
sturdier cat with a rounder face and longer fur. Havanas
are active and intelligent, with the British version rather
noisier than their American cousin.

FURTHER INFORMATION

• The Havana's original name, until 1970, was the
Chestnut Brown Foreign Shorthair. The name 'Havana',
redolent of opulent cigars, perfectly describes the rich,
dark colour of these cats.

• The Havana is one of the few natural breeds of brown cat and is sometimes confused with the Brown Burmese.

Manx

BREED BASICS

Varieties: Rumpies (with only a small hollow where the tail should have been), Stumpies, Risers or Stubbies (with a residual tail), and Longies (with a certain amount of tail). **Colours:** Most recognized colours are permitted. **Coat Length:** Double, with thick short undercoat and slightly longer overcoat. **Type of Fur:** Coarse but glossy. **Markings:** Any recognized patterns are permitted. **Size:** Medium. **Characteristics:** Round head with short nose and large, round eyes. Ears fairly tall set high on head and angled slightly outwards, tapering to narrow, rounded tip. Body is strong and stocky with rump higher than shoulders. Hind legs longer than forelegs, legs very well muscled. Paws are large and round, and pad colour should conform to that of the coat.

Tailless cats may have swum ashore on to the Isle of Man, off the west coast of England, from a wrecked Spanish vessel of the Armada in 1588; or they may have arrived on Phoenician trading ships from Japan 1000 years ago. It's more likely that the mutation occurred on the island about 400 years ago, and the island's isolation permitted the gene to be sustained. The truncated Manx tail results from an incomplete dominant gene, and the breed is at risk from spina bifida and fused vertebrae. If the Manx were not a historic breed we might be more critical of this dangerous abnormality. The Manx cat is the symbol of the Isle of Man, where it is depicted on coins and on tourist souvenirs of all kinds.

FURTHER INFORMATION

• When both parents are Rumpies, with no tail at all, it is likely that any kittens will die before birth. This occurs in about one quarter of Manx-Manx matings. Stumpies or Longies should always be used in a breeding programme.

• According to legend, the Manx cat was the last animal aboard the Ark, and lost its tail in the door when Noah slammed it in the face of the rising floods.

Rex

BREED BASICS

Varieties: Cornish Rex, Devon Rex, Selkirk Rex.
Colours: Many colours are recognized.
Coat Length: Very short. **Type of Fur:** In the Cornish Rex the guard hairs are absent, leaving coat short and plush, with ripple effect; the Devon Rex has all three types of hair, but severely distorted, leaving a curly soft coat; the Selkirk Rex has a thick plush coat with loose curls. **Markings:** Many different markings are recognized. **Size:** Medium, slight build.
Characteristics: Head medium wedge-shaped with oval eyes and large ears. Crinkled whiskers. Coat flattens when wet and regains curl slowly. Legs long and straight with small oval paws.

The first Rex cats reported, born in the 1930s, were regarded as freaks, but gradually tastes changed and when a curly coated kitten called Kallibunker was born in Cornwall, England in the early 1950s, it was regarded as a desirable novelty. Two of Kallibunker's offspring were sent to the USA in 1957 and founded the breed there. A few years later, a curly coated cat was found living in Devon, England. Although the two cats were geographically very close, each line was an independent mutation: if a Cornish Rex is mated with a Devon Rex, only straight-haired kittens result. Today, three Rex breeds are kept as domestic pets, all of which have the characteristic short, crimped coat of the breed. They are impish in character and make excellent pets.

FURTHER INFORMATION

• Rexes have extremely fine fur which does not shed much, causing less reaction in people with allergies. They are also susceptible to extremes of temperature.

• However, their normal body temperature is a degree higher than most other breeds, with a correspondingly faster metabolism and bigger appetite.

Scottish Fold

BREED BASICS

Varieties: None. **Colours:** Any of the 23 American
Shorthair colours are recognized.
Coat Length: Can be long- or short-coated.
Type of Fur: Soft and dense. **Markings:** Many
markings and patterns are recognized.
Size: Medium, compact. **Characteristics:** Round face
with round eyes and ears folded tightly forward to the
head. Eye colour should match the coat. Body
powerful and stocky. Short, sturdy legs.

In 1961, a kitten was born on a Perthshire farm with
ears which folded flat on its head. The farmer,
William Ross, decided to start a breeding line, and thus
the Scottish Fold was established. The breed was
recognized for championship status in America in 1978,
and the main centre for breeding is still the United
States. Scottish Folds must be mated to cats with
normal ears or the result is likely to be deformities of
the joints and cartilages, and although breeders insist
the folded ears cause no discomfort to the cats, there
have been fears that the breed may be prone to ear mites
and deafness. Folds are placid and good-natured.

FURTHER INFORMATION

• Scottish Fold kittens are born with normal, pointed ears.
The tips of the ears start to fold down at about two weeks.

• In every litter born to a Fold parent, there will be some kittens with this mutation.

There were once so many cats at the Houses of Parliament that a census was ordered to be taken. Only five were eventually found to have unimpeachable residential qualifications.

Ocicat

BREED BASICS

Varieties: Chocolate, Usual, Silver.
Colours: Tawny, silver, blue, golden, chocolate, lavender. **Coat Length:** Short. **Type of Fur:** Soft and light. **Markings:** Well defined pattern of spots over all the body. **Size:** Medium to large. **Characteristics:** Pointed face with large eyes and ears. Eyes should not be blue. Tail long and tapering to black tip. 'M' shaped mark on forehead. Long legs. Muscular, powerful body, especially apparent in kittens.

Ocicats are a relatively recent breed. A chance mating between a male Chocolate Point Siamese and a female Abyssinian/Seal Point Siamese resulted in an attractively spotted kitten born in 1964 in Michigan, USA, and the owner, Virginia Daly, set out to develop the bloodline. American shorthairs have been used in the USA to develop this breed. In Europe, the first kitten, bred from separate stock, was not born until 1984.

FURTHER INFORMATION

• These wild cat look-alikes were originally called 'Accicats', describing their accidental ancestry, then 'Ocelettes', describing their similarity to the ocelot.
• Championship status was granted in the USA by the CFA in 1987.

• Despite their wild appearance, Ocicats are as sweet-natured and obliging as any domestic breed.

Russian

BREED BASICS

Varieties: Blue, Black and White.
Coat Length: Short. **Type of Fur:** Double coat, with dense undercoat, plush fur with a texture reminiscent of a seal's coat. **Markings:** None. **Size:** Medium.
Characteristics: Body long and graceful but well-muscled. Short, wedge-shaped head with prominent whisker pads, and large, wide-set almond-shaped eyes, emerald green in colour. Ears are large and pointed, wide-set on the head with little furnishing. The nose and paw pads should match the body colour. The tail is long and tapering.

These cats were originally known as 'Archangel' cats, named after the northern Russian port from which they were brought to Britain by visiting sailors 300 or so years ago. At the early cat shows in Britain, they were shown with British Shorthairs, and it was not until 1912 that they were classed separately. Originally only available as Blues, Black and White forms are being developed, and are most popular in Australia and New Zealand.

FURTHER INFORMATION

• Trying to bolster declining numbers of Russians after the Second World War, Blue Point Siameses were used for breeding. This resulted in cats with a more foreign appearance, and latterly breeders have been working hard at re-creating their traditional features.

• Cats similar to Russians are still to be found in the northern regions of Russia and Scandinavia.

John Locke, an English sailor aboard a Venetian vessel bound for the Holy Land in 1553, witnessed the ship's cat fall overboard. He wrote: 'The shippes Cat… kept herself very valiantly above water, the which the master knowing, he caused the Skiffe with halfe a dozen men to fetch her again, when she was almost halfe a mile from the shippe. I hardly believe they would have made such haste and meanes if one of the company had bene in the like perill.'

Exotic Shorthair

BREED BASICS

Varieties: Over 50 varieties are permitted, with all the colours and patterns found in Persians and American Shorthairs. **Coat Length:** Medium; slightly longer than most other Shorthairs. **Type of Fur:** Soft and plushy, sufficiently dense to stand slightly away from the body. **Size:** Medium to large.

Characteristics: Short, cobby body with strong appearance. Round head with full cheeks and short nose. Ears are small and round-tipped. Eyes are large and round, with colour to match coat. Tail is short with a blunt tip, and is normally carried low. Paws are rounded with toes carried close, five in front, four behind.

Exotic Shorthairs were developed in the 1960s as a short-haired type of Persian for those who were attracted by the Persian cat but who did not want the responsibility of maintaining a long flowing coat. Parents must be one Persian and one American Shorthair, two Exotic Shorthairs, or one Persian and one Exotic

Shorthair. In common with most hybrids, the breed is extremely hardy and robust, combining the irresistible body shape and round face of the Persian with soft, plush coat. They also combine the best of the temperaments of the two parent breeds, being affectionate and calm.

FURTHER INFORMATION

• These cats should have no feathery fur. Their coats should be crisp and dense, and their ears should not be excessively furry.

Cats are sometimes thought to be psychic, but their seemingly uncanny ability to detect disturbances before we do is caused by their extremely acute hearing. Cats can perceive high-frequency sounds up to 65 kHz (65,000 cycles per second). Humans can perceive only up to about 20 kHz.

Malayan

BREED BASICS
Colours: Champagne, Blue, Platinum.
Coat Length: Short. **Type of Fur:** Thick and soft.
Markings: None. **Size:** Medium.
Characteristics: Long sleek body. Golden eyes. Faults
are blue or green eyes, a kinky tail, or white markings
on the body.

The Malayan is a very recent breed, officially recognized in the USA only in 1980. They are very similar to the Burmese, differing only in colour: only sable coloured cats are classed as Burmese, while cats of a champagne, blue or platinum colour are classed as Malayan. In Great Britain, all cats of Burmese type are classed as Burmese, with many different colours acceptable. In addition, the show standards vary throughout the world, with the Americans preferring a more rounded head and eyes.

FURTHER INFORMATION

• Malayan kittens can be born of Burmese parents. This is because they share the same genes, all being descended from Wong Mau, the Burmese cat brought back to the USA by Dr Joseph Thompson, the US Navy psychiatrist who founded the line in 1930.

Cats eat grass because it is good for them. Grass contains vitamins which they may need to assist in the manufacture of haemoglobin, and is also an emetic, helping them to regurgitate fur balls. If your cat has no access to grass, it might be a good idea to grow some in a window box for him.

Oriental Shorthair

BREED BASICS

Varieties: Solid, shaded, smoke, tabby, and parti-coloured coats are permitted.

Colours: In the USA 26 colours are permitted; in Great Britain many more. **Coat Length:** Short.

Type of Fur: Close-lying, fine and glossy.

Markings: A wide variety of markings.

Size: Medium. **Characteristics:** Blue eyes are preferred, but green or gold eyes are permitted in the USA. Body is svelte and lithe with slender legs and a narrow tail. The head is long and pointed, with large ears set far apart and pricked. Legs are long and slender with small oval paws. Tail is long and tapering. Nose leather, eye rims and paw pads to match coat colour.

Oriental Shorthairs do not necessarily come from the Orient: the name refers to breeds with the same slender physique, pointed head and slanted eyes. These cats are essentially Siamese cats without the colourpoint markings. The breed was developed in the 1950s. In Great

Britain each new colour was referred to as an individual breed, collectively called Foreign Shorthairs, but since 1991 all Siamese-derived breeds are termed 'Oriental'. In the USA they are known as Oriental Shorthairs and are judged as one breed. Orientals have many of the same characteristics as Siamese cats, being very talkative and demanding.

FURTHER INFORMATION

Most blue-eyed white cats are deaf, but the Foreign White can hear perfectly well.

The home range of a tom cat is about ten times the size of that of a female, a little less for a neutered tom. Females stay where there is enough food: but toms must overlap the home ranges of as many female cats as they can. Well-fed suburban cats have smaller ranges than hungry ferals.

Siamese

BREED BASICS

Varieties: Seal point, Blue point, Chocolate point, Lilac point, Cinnamon point, Caramel point, Fawn point, Tabby point, Tortie Point.

Colourpoint: Newer colourpoints, produced by recessive and dilute genes, are: Red point, Cream point, Seal Tortie point, Blue Tortie point, Chocolate Tortie point, Lilac Tortie point. **Colours:** Cream, white, blue, pale chocolate, pale grey base coat with darker points. Bib, chest and belly to be pale.

Coat Length: Short. **Type of Fur:** Close-fitting and fine. **Markings:** Pale coat shading to darker colourpoints on the face, ears, legs, and tail.

Size: Medium.

Characteristics: Sleek, athletic build with long body and legs, hind legs slightly longer than forelegs. Triangular head with almond-shaped, slanting, blue eyes. Ears are large and pricked, and should be set wide on the head to follow the line of the wedge. At night their eyes shine red instead of the usual green. Siamese cats tend towards poor health. Tail long and tapering.

Harrison Weir assessed the Siamese thus: 'Among the beautiful varieties of the domestic cat brought into notice by the cat shows, none deserves more attention than "the Royal Cat of Siam".' These fascinating animals were once restricted to the royal household and temples of Siam. In 1884 the King of Siam gave two Siamese cats to the British Consul-General in Bangkok, who took them home and exhibited them at the Crystal Palace. By 1892 the first breed standard had been written. Interestingly, the kink in the tail which today is regarded

as a fault was then part of the standard. Some early cats also had the squint which has also now been bred out. In the USA the Siamese line was nearly wiped out once by feline leukaemia and by bad breeding habits, but today it has recovered and breeders are much more careful. Siamese cats are highly intelligent, inquisitive animals, famously noisy and demanding.

FURTHER INFORMATION

• All Siamese kittens are white at birth and develop their markings gradually.
• Siamese cats have reduced pigment production in the hair fibres on the hotter parts of the body, with more pigment being produced at the cooler areas – the points.

• There are many charming stories connected to the royal origins of Siamese cats. The royal princesses of Siam were said to have kept their rings on the cat's tail, where a kink developed to stop them from falling off.

• Another story has it that these cats were set to guard Buddha's sacred golden goblet, and stared so intently at it that their eyes crossed.

Tonkinese

BREED BASICS

Varieties: Recognized in the USA are: Natural Mink, Blue Mink, Honey Mink, Champagne Mink, Platinum Mink. In Britain a new standard allows for all recognized Burmese colours.

Colours: Brown, bluish-grey, ruddy, beige, silver.

Coat Length: Medium short. **Type of Fur:** Soft and thick, close-lying and with a natural sheen similar to the coat of a mink. **Markings:** Dark points like a Siamese. **Size:** Medium. **Characteristics:** A triangular head with blue-green, almond-shaped eyes and large ears set wide on the head. The body is strong, not as sleek as that of a Siamese, but with long legs. The hind legs are longer than the forelegs. Paws are oval and the paw pads should harmonize with the coat colour. The tail is long in proportion to the body and should taper.

This is a new name for an old breed, the ancient Copper cat of south-east Asia. The Tonkinese is a cross between the Siamese and the Burmese, but the modern breed was developed in Canada in the 1960s, retaining the dark coat of the Burmese and with the visibly darker points of the Siamese. It was given championship status in 1984. Tonkinese cats have exceptionally inquisitive natures and are extremely energetic. In addition they are famous for their hunting prowess. Tonkinese are late developers, and are not at their best until over two years old.

FURTHER INFORMATION

• The varieties of Tonkinese are known as 'mink' because the cats' fur is so exceptionally soft and dense, with a wonderful sheen. The coat can take up to sixteen months to develop fully, and even then can continue to improve.

• The breed still only has provisional status in the UK and Europe.

There is a Thai belief that the soul of a spiritually enlightened person enters a cat until the animal dies too. Long ago, at the death of a Thai monarch, his favourite cat would be buried with him, though with a small hole left from which the cat might emerge. When it did, it was held to embody the king's spirit.

Burmilla

BREED BASICS

Varieties: Standard, Silver. **Colours:** Silver or golden ground colour tipped with black, or any standard colour. In Silvers, the colours may be reduced in intensity. **Coat Length:** Medium short.
Type of Fur: Soft and dense. **Markings:** Some light spotting on the belly, and traces of tabby marking. An 'M' on the forehead. Tail should be lightly marked with a solid tip. **Size:** Medium.
Characteristics: Strong body, with a round head and short nose, terracotta in colour. Eyes are half way between round and almond-shaped, and are green in colour. Ears are medium in size and forward-tilting. The tail is medium in length and should taper to a blunt tip. The tail is usually carried slightly up. The legs are slim, with the hind legs longer than the forelegs. The paws are oval in shape with black pads.

The Burmilla is a Burmese/Chinchilla cross, developed in Britain from the chance mating of a Lilac Burmese queen and a Chinchilla tom in 1981. The resulting four kittens were the breed's founders, and a Burmilla Cat Club was established in 1984. It has yet to be officially recognized, but is becoming increasingly popular none the less. The breed is docile and good-natured and makes an excellent pet.

FURTHER INFORMATION

• The colour of the tipping is not constant throughout a cat's life, and will tend to darken as the cat ages. Kittens are born with light colouration.

The basic cat is a tabby in colouring, and all cats would look alike were it not for mutation. Even selfs are really tabby, but their markings are hidden by the breeds' genetic make-up.

Bengal

BREED BASICS

Colours: Brown, Charcoal, Snow.
Coat Length: Medium short. **Type of Fur:** Soft and dense. **Markings:** Underparts paler than the rest of the body, over which are rosette spots and clear lines. **Size:** Medium. **Characteristics:** Strong body, with a narrow wedge-shaped head and short nose, terracotta in colour with a black liner. Eyes are half way between round and almond-shaped, and are green in colour. Ears are medium in size with rounded tips. The tail is medium in length. The legs are strong with rounded paws.

The Bengal, a cross between the Asian leopard cat of southern Asia and domestic shorthairs, is a new breed, developed in the United States in the 1970s after a research programme into the Asian leopard cat's natural immunity to feline leukaemia. The Bengal combines beautiful 'wild' tawny colouring and marking with the trusting nature of the domestic cat. Bengals are playful and quick-witted, in appearance every inch the wild hunter yet quietly at home in a human household. Bengals are excellent mousers and popular on farms. They are equally popular as city pets because of their nature, although they can be temperamental. Bengals have been exhibited at most major cat shows in Britain, but to date no Standard of Points has been fully ratified by the GCCF.

FURTHER INFORMATION

• The Asian leopard cat is a small wild cat weighing only about 4.5kg/10lb. It inhabits the forests of Southern Asia and has a beautifully marked, dense pelt.

• Other wild cats, such as ocelots or margays, have found their way into homes as pets, and there are many recorded instances of wild cats successfully cross-breeding with domestic cats.

California Spangled

BREED BASICS

Colours: Silver, Bronze, Black, White, Charcoal, Gold, Red, Blue, Brown. **Coat Length:** Short.
Type of Fur: Soft and sleek.
Markings: Rosette spots and stripes all over.
Size: Medium. **Characteristics:** Muscular, lean body, with a medium head and strong jaw and chin and almond-shaped eyes. Ears are medium in size with rounded tips, set well back on the head. Legs are strong, with large paws. Fur is longer on the underparts. The tail is well-furred, with a black tip.

The California Spangled is the ultimate in designer cats. It was created in the mid-1980s by the American breeder and

TV writer Paul Casey, who launched the breed in the 1986 Christmas catalogue of the New York department store Neiman Marcus. Casey's aim, in crossing eight separate bloodlines, among them a Siamese and a spotted silver Angora, was to satisfy the demand for spotted cats and thus to take the pressure off wild breeds. Casey's breeding programme began in 1971 and the spotted pattern took five generations to develop. This breed is sociable and active, and makes an ideal family pet.

FURTHER INFORMATION

• There is a waiting list for California Spangled kittens, and the asking price is said to be around $3500 each.

Chartreux

BREED BASICS
Colours: Blue-grey only.
Coat Length: Short. **Type of Fur:** Dense and glossy.
Markings: Solid blue colour with silver tipping.
Size: Medium. **Characteristics:** Stocky, muscular body,
with large trapezoid head. Eyes are round and orange
in colour. Ears are medium in size with rounded tips.
Nose leather is dark blue. Tail is medium in length;
rounded paws.

In Britain, the Chartreux is extremely close in type to the British Blue Shorthair and no distinction is made between them. In North America it has had its own class since the 1970s. The Chartreux is thought to have been developed from North African cats in the Middle Ages by Carthusian monks at the monastery of La Grande Chartreuse in France, otherwise famous for its aromatic liqueur. The breed made its way to North America in 1970, where it is still rare. Chartreux are gentle and quiet, and can become very attached to their owners.

FURTHER INFORMATION
• The earliest recorded use of the name Chartreux was in 1723 when the *Universal Dictionary of Commerce* used the name to describe cats with blue fur.
• The Leger sisters of Brittany in France are the first

people known to have shown Chartreux cats, which they did in Paris in 1931.

LONGHAIRED
～ BREEDS ～

Introduction

Wild cats generally have short, practical fur, as do most domestic ones. Longhaired cats have existed in certain parts of the world for many centuries, but have only been known in Europe since the 16th century. Most of today's longhaired breeds are the descendants of longhaired cats brought back to Europe from Turkey and Persia in the 19th century. The original Persian cats

looked very different from the cat we call Persian today. Their faces were much longer, and their coats were shorter than that of the modern cat.

Today most cats of the long-hair type are known in Britain as Longhairs, and each colour is classified as a separate breed. In the USA, these cats are all called Persians, and the colours are listed as varieties.

There are various longhaired cats which are not of the Persian type, most of which come from cold climates where a thick, long coat is essential. These types, for example the Norwegian Forest Cat and the Maine Coon, have dense undercoats and long guard hairs, and require very little grooming despite the length of their fur. These cats tend also to have a different body shape from that of the Persian, with slimmer legs and trunks, narrower faces and longer noses.

Although longhaired cats do look gorgeous and feel luxurious to stroke, their fur sheds copiously and will require frequent vacuuming from your carpets and armchairs!

Balinese

BREED BASICS

Varieties/Colours: Lilac point, Blue point, Chocolate point, Seal Tortie point are recognized by the CFA for championship status. Other variants (known in the USA as Javanese): Seal point, Seal Tortie Tabby point, Chocolate Tortie point, Red Tabby point, Blue tabby point, Seal Tabby point, Chocolate Tabby point. **Coat Length:** Medium long, but shorter than most other longhaired breeds. **Type of Fur:** Fine and silky with no undercoat. Relatively non-matting and with a tendency to curl. **Markings:** Siamese-type points on face, ears, paws, legs and tail. **Size:** Medium. **Characteristics:** Wedge-shaped head with almond-shaped blue eyes. Ears large and pricked with width at the base, set to follow the line of the head. Ears may be tufted. Body is slender and strong with slim legs. Forelegs shorter than the hind legs. Feet small and oval. The tail is long, with well-plumed fur, free from any kink.

The first Balinese kittens, looking like longhaired Siamese, were born to Siamese parents in California in the 1940s. They were the result of a spontaneous mutation, probably because of a recessive gene inherent in some American Siamese bloodlines, but also possibly because longhaired Angoras had been occasionally paired with Siamese in Great Britain in the 1920s. US organizations have recognized the breed since the 1960s, and in the UK the breed has been recognized since the 1980s. Balinese are lively and spirited, but are not quite as talkative and boisterous as Siamese.

FURTHER INFORMATION

• In Europe, breeders frequently use Angoras as well as Siamese in their breeding programmes in order to keep the coat length of this breed.

• At first Balinese cats were known as Longhaired Siamese, but as the breed became established their graceful gait called to breeders' minds the swaying native dancers of the island of Bali, and the new name of Balinese emerged.

Birman

BREED BASICS

Varieties: Seal point, Cream point, Red point, Lilac point, Blue point, Chocolate point, Seal Tortie point, Blue Tortie Point, Chocolate Tortie Point, Lilac Tortie Point, Seal Tabby Point, Blue Tabby Point, Chocolate Tabby Point, Lilac Tabby Point, Red Tabby Point, Cream Tabby Point, Seal Tortie Tabby point, Blue Tortie Tabby point, Chocolate Tortie Tabby Point, Lilac Tortie Tabby Point. **Colours:** Distinguishing colours are those of the Siamese. Body colour of gold-cream or milk-white with Siamese-type points. **Coat Length:** Long, full ruff round neck, slightly curled on stomach. **Type of Fur:** Fine and silky, slightly curly on stomach and resistant to snarls. **Markings:** Even, Siamese-type colour points. **Size:** Medium. **Characteristics:** Strong, stocky body with thick-set legs. Paws are large and round, with white boots. On the rear paws the boots extend up the back legs. Head is rounded with medium-sized, round-tipped ears. Eyes are blue, almost round and slightly slanted. The tail is medium in length and bushy, with long fine hair.

Birmans have a highly romantic history. They were sacred cats at the subterranean temples of Lao-Tsun in north-east Burma, where a British Army officer saw them in 1885. It is said that long ago an army of Thais invaded the temple complex and killed the priest, Mun-Ha. One of the sacred cats, Sinh by name, leapt on to the body. Immediately his feet, purified by their contact, became pure white, and his eyes changed from yellow to sapphire blue. At the same time his white back was transformed to gold. The other priests were inspired by this miracle and went on to rout their enemies. Later it was found that all the other sacred cats now carried the new markings too. Birmans are gentle and intelligent and make ideal pets in quiet households.

FURTHER INFORMATION

• In 1919 two Birman cats were said to have been sent to France by the Buddhist priests in gratitude for help received against their enemies. Only the female survived the journey, but she had a litter of kittens soon after her arrival, and so the breed became established in Europe.

• The breed was established in France in 1925, in Britain in 1966, and in the USA in 1967.

• The Birman's luxurious coat requires regular grooming.

Cymric

BREED BASICS
Colours: All colours and patterns are accepted.
Coat Length: Medium to long. **Type of Fur:** Smooth
and thick with a heavy undercoat. **Size:** Medium.
Characteristics: Strong, stocky body like the Manx.
Rounded head with full cheeks and small ears. Eyes
rounded and of a colour to suit coat. Hind legs longer
than front legs, giving rise to the typical Manx
hopping, 'rabbit' gait.

The Cymric, whose name means 'Welsh', is a
longhaired variety of the Manx cat from the Isle of
Man. The breed was developed from a longhaired
kitten born to a Manx mother in Canada in the 1960s.
In common with Manx cats, it is said that too much
breeding of these tailless cats produces lethal genetic
deformities so cats with tails (however vestigial) must
continue to be used in breeding programmes. Only a
few organizations accept the Cymric but the breed's
standards have been established. Cymric are docile and
intelligent and seem to enjoy being indoors.

FURTHER INFORMATION
• Cymrics are rare in the UK but are popular in the USA.
• The only type of Manx or Cymric cat recognized for
showing in the UK is the Rumpy, with no tail at all.

Javanese

BREED BASICS
Varieties: Cinnamon. **Colours:** Tawny brown.
Coat Length: Medium to long, shorter on the sides of
the body and head. **Type of Fur:** Fine and silky.
Markings: None. **Size:** Medium.
Characteristics: Slender, graceful body with long slim
legs. Head is wedge-shaped with a straight nose. Eyes
slant towards the nose, and ears are large and wide.
Tail is long and plumy.

In North America, the name Javanese is used to
describe the varieties of Balinese which do not
correspond to the four traditional Siamese
point-colours. In New Zealand, it is the self and spotted
varieties of the Balinese which are called Javanese. In
Great Britain, however, the Javanese is a separate breed,
developed in an attempt to recreate the Angora. The
breed was granted championship status in 1984.
Javanese are affectionate and gentle.

FURTHER INFORMATION
• The Javanese has only recently been introduced into
the USA, but already there is one Supreme Grand
Champion.

An Irish monk of the eighth or ninth century wrote
this delightful poem to his cat:

I and Pangur Ban, my cat
'Tis a like task we are at;
Hunting mice is his delight
Hunting words I sit all night,
So in peace our tasks we play,
Pangur Ban, my cat, and I.

Maine Coon

BREED BASICS

Varieties: Apart from Chocolate, Lilac or Siamese-type patterns, the Maine Coon is bred in every colour and coat pattern. **Coat Length:** Medium.
Type of Fur: Thick and shaggy double-coat, softer to the touch than it appears. During the cold New England winters, the cat develops a thick ruff round the neck. **Size:** Large. The male Maine Coon can weigh around 9.1kg/20 lb. **Characteristics:** Extremely strong, muscular body, with powerful legs and large round paws. and a broad chest. The head is medium in length, rounded with round eyes and large tall ears, wide at the base and tapering to appear pointed at the tip. The tail is long with a good plume. Ears feathered and tufted, paws tufted.

The Maine Coon is North America's oldest indigenous breed. Its home is the state of Maine, New England, where early frontiersmen believed these large cats were the result of breeding between a domestic cat and a racoon. The longhair gene probably arrived with immigrant cats, but it may be that Maine Coons actually arrived with the Vikings from their Greenland or Iceland trading posts – a Norse coin from the 11th century has been found in Maine, and the skins of cats are known to have been valuable in trade. Feral cats could easily have survived down the years to integrate with later settlers' cats. The breed was given official recognition in the USA in 1967, having been out of fashion since its first showing at the Madison Square Cat Show of 1895. Maine Coons are extremely robust, boisterous and independent, and are alert, capable hunters. They need plenty of space and if given it, seldom suffer from behavioural problems of any kind. Their rugged weatherproof coat does not need constant grooming, which helps to make these cats easier to look after than Longhairs of the Persian type.

FURTHER INFORMATION

• Because of their wild origins, Maine Coons are happy to sleep almost anywhere and do not require coddling.

• They are also well-known for the extraordinary chirruping noise they make, quite unlike a normal meow or purr.

• The Maine Coon was recognized in the USA as early as 1967, but not in the UK until the 1980s.

Norwegian Forest Cat

BREED BASICS

Varieties: All coat colours and patterns are acceptable, with or without white, except chocolate, lilac and Siamese patterns. **Coat Length:** Semi-long.
Type of Fur: Double. A thick undercoat is covered by smooth, water-resistant outer fur. In winter the cat has a shirt-front, a full ruff, and knickerbockers.
Size: Medium. **Characteristics:** Strong body with long powerful legs (hind legs longer than front legs), and tufts between toes. Large, heavy paws, with pads corresponding in colour to coat. Head is triangular with full cheeks and prominent whiskers. Eyes are almond-shaped. Ears are large and abundantly tufted. Tail is long and heavily furred, reaching at least to the shoulder blade, and generally carried high. Claws are extremely strong, allowing easy climbing over rock as well as trees.

The Norsk Skaukatt, or Norwegian Forest Cat, is the native cat of Norway, and the northern race of the European Wild Cat.

These wild-looking cats roam and hunt freely through Norway's large, cold forests, as well as living happy domestic lives alongside humans. They have a dense, warm undercoat and a coarse overcoat which sheds even the heaviest rain and snow. They are extremely agile and strong, inventive and independent. They are great climbers and are exceptionally strong. They are affectionate and intelligent, enjoying human company. Norwegian Forest Cats are said to mature slowly, taking up to four years to reach adulthood.

FURTHER INFORMATION

• First shown in 1938, pedigree breeding of the Norwegian Forest Cat dwindled during the Second World War, and was not revived until the 1970s.
• The breed has been recognized in Europe, but has yet to achieve this status in the USA.
• Cats prowl through many Scandinavian fairy tales and myths as fairies and fairy companions. The goddess Freya drove a chariot pulled by giant cats, and enchanted cats roamed the dark, impenetrable forests.

Ragdoll

BREED BASICS

Patterns: Bi-colour, Colourpoint, Mitted.
Colours: Seal point, Chocolate point, Blue point,
Lilac point. **Coat Length:** Medium. Longer around
the neck, short over the shoulders, medium on back,
sides, abdomen and hindquarters, short to medium on
front legs. **Type of Fur:** Very dense and silky.
Markings: Usual markings for bi-colours and
colourpoints are recognized, with good contrast
required. **Size:** Very large: males can weigh up to
9.1kg/20lb. **Characteristics:** The body is strong and
muscular, with a short neck, deep chest and medium,
stocky legs. The head tapers, with full cheeks and oval
blue eyes. Ears are medium in size and tilt slightly
forward, with medium tufts and
rounded tips. Paws are large, round
and tufted, with dark brown or
black pads. Tail is long and bushy.

Ragdolls were developed in the
USA in the 1960s by a breeder
who was trying to cultivate a
good, gentle temperament. The
breeder succeeded, and Ragdolls
are now famous for their unique
characteristic of relaxing
completely when they are

touched or picked up. This characteristic is probably the result of a genetic mutation. It is a myth that they feel no pain, however; breeders are adamant that Ragdolls have the same pain threshold as any other cat. They are extremely docile and gentle, and make ideal pets.

FURTHER INFORMATION

• The Ragdoll was the first breed of cat in history to receive its own trademark.

• Its early development was strictly controlled by the original breeder, using a franchise system.

• The first Ragdoll kittens were born to a white Persian queen who had suffered a broken pelvis in a car accident. A myth grew up that her kittens could not feel pain, but it is definitely not the case.

Somali

BREED BASICS

Pattern: Ticked coat, with at least three bands of colour on each hair: Tortie, Silver, Tortie Silver. **Colours:** Usual, Sorrel, Chocolate, Blue, Lilac, Fawn, Red, Cream. **Coat Length:** Medium-long, with ruff and full breeches. **Type of Fur:** Fine and silky, resistant to tangling. **Markings:** Ticked tabby fur. **Size:** Medium. **Characteristics:** Elegant, long body with long slender legs. Head is wedge-shaped with almond-shaped eyes, amber, hazel or green in colour with dark lid skin. Ears are large and pointed, set well apart. Nose pad is pink. Paws are oval, with tufted pads. Tail is medium in length with full plume.

These cats are a long-haired variety of the Abyssinian cat. They are named for Somalia, a neighbouring country to Ethiopia, to emphasize their similarity to Abyssinians. Although the longhaired cat is a natural genetic mutation, the breed was developed in the United States during

the 1960s, and by 1978 the Somali was recognized by all American governing bodies. It was recognized in Great Britain in 1983 and received championship status in 1991. The breed is now very popular throughout Europe and even as far afield as Australia. Somalis are good tempered but are very vocal and can be demanding. They can be trained to do tricks or walk on a lead; they are very active and should not be kept exclusively indoors.

FURTHER INFORMATION

• The short hair of the Abyssinian has two or three bands of ticking, but the longer, shaggy hair of the Somali can carry as many as ten or more bands of colour, giving a rich colouration.

Tiffanie

BREED BASICS
Patterns: Self, Tortie. **Colours:** Sable, Red,
Blue-tipped Silver, Black, Blue, Chocolate, Lilac,
Caramel, Apricot, Cream. **Coat Length:** Long, with a
ruff round the neck. **Type of Fur:** Very fine.
Size: Medium. **Characteristics:** Body is more muscular
and stocky than that of a Siamese, with long slim legs.
Paws are oval with brown pads. Head is rounded with
round eyes, golden in colour. Ears are medium in size
and slightly rounded at the tip. The tail is medium in
length and bushy.

The Tiffanie was developed as a long-haired version
of the Burmese during the 1970s. Despite its
elegance, it is not widely known, and has still to be
recognized by any organization. The Tiffanie is not an
easy cat to breed. The recessive longhair gene means
that very few longhaired cats are born in each litter.
They are inquisitive, vocal and playful.

FURTHER INFORMATION
• The Tiffanie may well increase in popularity as more
colours are developed by breeders.
• Breeders are also increasing the use of good Burmese
cats in their breeding programmes in order to develop a
cat more like a longhaired Burmese in type.

Cats are said to increase their grooming when they have been out in the sun. This is because the action of sunlight produces extra Vitamin D, and cats are able to acquire this essential vitamin by licking their fur.

Angora

BREED BASICS

Varieties: Self, Tortoiseshell, Smoke, Tabby, Silver Tabby, Silver Tortie Tabby. **Colours:** White, Black, Blue, Chocolate, Lilac, Red, Cream, Cinnamon, Caramel, Fawn. **Coat Length:** Medium-long. **Type of Fur:** Very fine with a tendency to curl. No thick undercoat, so less grooming is required than that of a Persian. **Size:** Medium.

Characteristics: Elegant, lithe body with long slim legs. Paws are small with toe tufts. Head is small in proportion to the body, wedge-shaped with large, almond-shaped eyes, green in colour except for blue-eyed and odd-eyed Whites. Ears are large and pricked. Tail is long and fluffy, carried up.

The Angora is one of the oldest cat breeds coming from Ancient Turkey. It could have been one of the first longhaired cats to come to Europe but was less popular than the sturdier Persian. Today they are more oriental in build and looks, and are also very vocal. The CFA recognized the breed in the 1970s. Angoras are gentle and friendly, and are capable of long periods of inactivity when they like nothing better than to lie asleep in a warm comfortable bed.

FURTHER INFORMATION

• The first American Angoras were also white, and they suffered from the deafness so common in white cats.

Turkish Angora

BREED BASICS

Varieties: Self, Tortoiseshell, Tabby.
Colours: White, Black, Blue, Cream.
Coat Length: Medium-long. **Type of Fur:** Very fine with a tendency to curl. No thick undercoat, so less grooming is required than that of a Persian.
Size: Medium. **Characteristics:** Elegant, lithe body with long slim legs. Paws are small with toe tufts.
Head is small in proportion to the body, wedge-shaped with large, almond-shaped eyes, green in colour except for blue-eyed and odd-eyed Whites. Ears are large and pricked. Tail is long and fluffy, carried up.

The Angora is probably a distant cousin of the Persian, but the two lines developed separately over the years, with the Angora becoming established in Ankara, the capital of Turkey. Angoras sent to France and Italy in the 16th century as diplomatic gifts from the Sultan were the first long-haired cats in Europe. At first they were very popular, but later lost ground to Persians and the new Longhairs and the breed went into a severe decline. In the early 1960s, a breeding pair was bought from Ankara Zoo and taken to the USA, where a breeding programme was developed and sparked new interest.

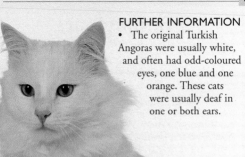

FURTHER INFORMATION
• The original Turkish Angoras were usually white, and often had odd-coloured eyes, one blue and one orange. These cats were usually deaf in one or both ears.

Turkish Van

BREED BASICS

Varieties: Auburn and white, Cream and white, Black and white, Tortoiseshell and white.
Coat Length: Long. Winter coat is longer than summer coat. **Type of Fur:** Fine and silky with no undercoat. **Markings:** The coat is white with darker markings in the recognized colours on the face and tail. **Size:** Medium. **Characteristics:** Body is strongly-muscled, with medium length legs. Paws are small, with toe tufts and pink pads. The head is wedge-shaped with a pink nose pad and large oval eyes with pink rims. Ears are large and pointed with tufts. The tail is long and feathery.

The Turkish Van is unique among small cats in that it loves water and swims enthusiastically. It has been domesticated for several hundred years in the Lake Van region of Turkey, and perhaps learned to swim while trying to catch the fish in the lake. The Lake Van region suffers from extremes of temperature, and these cats have developed an immensely thick winter coat to protect themselves from the freezing weather. In summer the cat moults heavily, shedding nearly all its winter coat. Two Turkish Vans were brought back to Britain in the 1950s by a couple on holiday, who went on to establish the breed in the UK. Recognition was granted in 1969. Turkish Vans are highly intelligent and affectionate cats.

FURTHER INFORMATION

• Legend has it that the Turkish Van cats living locally at the town of Van are usually all-white, and usually have odd eyes, one green and one blue.

• The white patch in the centre of the forehead of the patched Turkish Van is said by the Turkish people to be the thumbprint of Allah.

American Curl

BREED BASICS

Varieties: Shorthaired American Curl.
Colours: Black, Black and white, Tabby and white,
and any other recognized colour.
Coat Length: Medium to long. **Type of Fur:** Silky,
scanty undercoat causes fur to lie close to body.
Markings: Any recognized patterns are acceptable.
Size: Medium. **Characteristics:** Stocky, muscular body
with sturdy legs, hind legs slightly longer than
forelegs. Head is rounded with rounded eyes. Tail is
long and plumy. Unique ears curl backwards, with
tufts within and at the tip.

The mutation which causes the ears of these cats to curl backwards creates a highly distinctive appearance. The original cat of the breed was a stray with this genetic deformity. John and Grace Ruga, cat breeders in California, USA, were charmed by her appearance and adopted her. When her first litter contained two kittens with curled ears, they realized they could establish a new breed, and thereafter preliminary acceptance in the USA was rapid. Curls are lively, adaptable and independent.

FURTHER INFORMATION

• Kittens are born with normal-looking ears. Typically, about half a litter will then develop curled ears, starting at about a week old. The curl continues to develop for several months until the ears are at an angle of about 90 degrees.

• Curled ears can be swivelled in the same way as a normal ear.

The National Cat Club was founded in Great Britain by Harrison Weir in 1887, and by 1893 the first official cat stud book had been started. Today there are about 65 annual shows in Britain and 400 in the United States.

Siberian Forest

BREED BASICS
Varieties: None. **Colours:** Usually tabby.
Coat Length: Long. **Type of Fur:** Dense waterproof
undercoat with long coarse guard hairs growing
through to shed water and snow. **Markings:** Tabby.
Size: Medium to large. **Characteristics:** Strong
powerful body with sturdy legs. Wedge-shaped head
with rounded eyes and large ears. Ruff round neck
and shaggy hindquarters. Tail is long and bushy.

These cats are very similar in appearance to Norwegian
Forest Cats, with their abundant coat for warmth
and protection in the harsh northern climate. They
have probably existed for thousands of years, a hardy,
resourceful breed independent of humans. Today there
is increasing interest in developing and formalizing the
breed, and as this takes place a wider variety of colours
and coat patterns is becoming acceptable. Siberian
Forest Cats need a great deal of exercise, and do not
thrive if kept in confined circumstances.

FURTHER INFORMATION
• Russian longhairs were shown at the early cat shows
arranged by Harrison Weir, who owned one himself.
• The Russian cat was then largely forgotten in the
West while 20th-century contact with Russia waned. In
1991 a Russian cat was exhibited at the International

Cat Show in New York by Olga Frolova, President of the Soviet Union's Cat Fancy.

 Longhaired cats are abundant throughout Scandinavia. Denmark and Sweden have their own versions, called the Racekatte and the Rugkatt respectively.

Persian Longhairs

In the USA these cats are all known as Persians and are considered to have many varieties, divided into five divisions for showing purposes: solid, shaded, smoke/tabby, parti-coloured and point-restricted colours. In Britain they are called Longhairs and each different colour is considered a separate breed, of which there are nearly 50. The earliest European record of longhaired cats comes from around the middle of the 16th century, when cats from the Angora region of Turkey were brought to Europe by traders and travellers. Other longhaired cats were brought to Europe from Persia, and with their extravagant, silky coats, they became immediately popular. Longhairs are quiet and undemanding, but they do require a considerable amount of grooming to keep their coats in tip-top condition. They should be brushed and groomed for at least 15 minutes each day to maintain the glamour of that beautiful coat, and to keep tangles at bay. Even the smallest snag can cause intense irritation to the sensitive Persian skin.

New Longhairs

New breeds are constantly being developed, among them the Golden, the Shaded Golden, the Shaded Silver, the Chinchilla Golden, the Lilac-Cream, the Chocolate Tortoiseshell, Golden Tabby, and Golden Tortie-Tabby (Torbie). All these new varieties show the gentle disposition customary in this type of cat. Their physique and fur type are as for all the other Longhairs.

Black Longhair

BREED BASICS
Varieties: None. **Colour:** Black.
Coat Length: Very long. Full frill on shoulders and
between front legs. **Type of Fur:** Fine and silky guard
hairs over a dense woolly undercoat.
Markings: The coat should be without shading,
marking or white hairs. **Size:** Medium.
Characteristics: A strong, cobby body with short thick
legs and large round paws, well tufted. The paw pads
should be black in the UK and black or brown in the
USA. The head is round with a short snub black nose
and large, rounded orange or copper coloured eyes.
The ears are short with round tips. The whiskers
should be long. The tail should be short and very
furry with a good plume.

FURTHER INFORMATION
• Black cats have not always been popular; for centuries
they were considered incarnations of Satan but today
the pure black colour is sought-after because it is so
difficult to achieve.
• Both sunlight and damp can adversely affect the coat
colour, causing lightening or 'rustiness'.
• In Brittany it was believed that every black cat has
one white hair. If one could find this hair and pluck it
out, it would be a powerful good luck charm.

Colourpoint Longhair

BREED BASICS

Varieties/Colours: All point colours are available, with the body being warm cream or ivory.

Coat Length: Long. **Type of Fur:** Very thick and soft.

Markings: Colourpoints as for Siamese.

Size: Medium to large. **Characteristics:** Body is cobby and strong, with short stocky legs. Paws are rounded with good tufts. The head is broad and rounded with a short nose and rounded eyes, which should be blue in colour. Ears are small and round-tipped. The whiskers should be very long. The tail should not be too long, and should be very full.

In the 1920s a Swedish geneticist, Dr Tjebbes, began a research study during which he crossed Siamese, Persian and Birman cats. The scientist was undertaking pure research, and was not intending to develop a new breed, but his work was continued in the USA during the 1930s and the first Colourpoint Longhair, a kitten named Debutante, was born in 1935. Breeders in Britain and the USA took up the programme and gradually developed this Siamese-marked, Persian-build cat. They are exceptionally beautiful cats, combining the luxurious coat of a Persian cat with the delicate markings of a Siamese. In the USA these cats are known as Himalayan. They are very affectionate and playful, and enjoy the company of humans.

FURTHER INFORMATION

• Colourpoint Longhairs were crossed with Burmese cats in an attempt to produce a solid chocolate Longhair. The resulting kittens were developed into the breed now called Tiffanie.

Superstition has it that warts can be removed by rubbing them with a male tortoiseshell cat's tail – but only in the month of May.

White Longhair

BREED BASICS

Varieties: Orange-eyed White, Blue-eyed White, Odd-eyed White. **Colour:** White.
Coat Length: Very long. **Type of Fur:** Fine and silky guard hairs over a dense woolly undercoat.
Markings: None permitted; coat should be pure white. **Size:** Medium. **Characteristics:** A strong, cobby body with short thick legs. The paw pads should be pink. The head is round with a short snub pink nose and large, rounded eyes. The ears are short with round tips. The whiskers should be long. The tail should be short and very furry with a good plume. In common with most white cats, the Blue-eyed White tends to be deaf. The Odd-eyed White is sometimes deaf on the blue-eyed side.

White was the colour of the original Angora cats living in their native Turkey, and the modern White Longhair was developed by crossing Angoras with Persians. The breed was first shown in London in 1903, and was recognized in the USA during the 1950s.

FURTHER INFORMATION

• Original Persians looked very different from modern cats. Their faces were longer and their coats neither so thick nor so luxurious. Colours also limited.
• Persians can have hair up to 10cm/4in long.

Blue Longhair

BREED BASICS

Varieties: None. **Colours:** Blue.
Coat Length: Very long. **Type of Fur:** Fine and silky
guard hairs over a dense woolly undercoat.
Markings: None permitted. Kittens often show tabby
markings at first. **Size:** Medium.
Characteristics: A strong, cobby body with short thick
legs. The paw pads, nose leather and eye rims should
be blue-grey. The head is round with a short snub
blue nose and large, rounded orange or
copper-coloured eyes. The ears are short with round
tips. The whiskers should be long. The tail should be
short and very furry with a good plume.

This delightful smoky colour is the result of crossing black with white cats, and is one of the earliest colours. It is still a perennial favourite, and Blues even have special shows dedicated solely to them.

FURTHER INFORMATION

• The Blue Persian Society was formed in Britain in 1901, and the breed characteristics were tightened up shortly thereafter.

• Early Blues often had green eyes, but soon only cats with copper-coloured eyes had a chance of winning.

• Queen Victoria was inseparable from her two blue Persians. This royal stamp of approval guaranteed the popularity of the breed.

Cream Longhair

BREED BASICS

Varieties: None. **Colours:** Pale cream or honey.
Coat Length: Very long. **Type of Fur:** Fine and silky
guard hairs over a dense woolly undercoat.
Markings: None. **Size:** Medium.
Country of Origin: Great Britain.
Characteristics: A strong, cobby body with short thick
legs. The paw pads, eye rims and nose leather should
be pink. The head is round with a short snub pink
nose and large, rounded orange or copper-coloured
eyes. The ears are short with round tips. The whiskers
should be long. The tail should be short and very
furry with a good plume.

The early Creams were considered to be only poor examples of Reds and as such were not prized in Britain. In the USA, however, they became popular, and a breeding programme was established there. They are now valuable and sought-after, with their opulent good looks.

FURTHER INFORMATION

• The Cream colour first appeared from an accidental crossing of Blue and Red Longhairs.

Red Longhair

BREED BASICS

Varieties: Peke-faced Red, Red Tabby.
Colours: Deep orange-red. **Coat Length:** Very long.
Type of Fur: Fine and silky guard hairs over a dense
woolly undercoat. **Markings:** None.
Size: Medium. **Country of Origin:** Great Britain.
Characteristics: A strong, cobby body with short thick
legs. The paw pads, eye rims and nose leather should
be brick-red. The head is round with a short snub
brick-red nose and large, rounded.orange or
copper-coloured eyes. The ears are short with round
tips. The whiskers should be long. The tail should be
short and very furry with a good plume.

The red colour was developed in England around the turn of the century, but the pure colour is relatively rare, tabby markings often coming through. The colour was originally known as 'Orange'.

FURTHER INFORMATION

• Peke-faced Reds appear spontaneously in some litters of Reds. Their squashed appearance is encouraged by some American breeders, but in Britain it is discouraged because the extreme shortness of the nose can cause breathing difficulties and other health problems for the cat.

Legend has it that the Persian cat was created by a magician from a little flicker of fire, the spark of two distant stars, and a swirl of grey smoke.

Blue-Cream Longhair

BREED BASICS

Varieties: None. **Colours:** Soft mixture of blue and cream. **Coat Length:** Very long. **Type of Fur:** Fine and silky guard hairs over a dense woolly undercoat. **Markings:** In the UK the standard requires that the colours mingle softly: in the USA clearly defined separate areas of colour are the requirement.

Size: Medium. **Characteristics:** A strong, cobby body with short thick legs. The paw pads should be blue. The head is round with a short snub blue nose and large, rounded copper-coloured eyes. The ears are short with round tips. The whiskers should be long. The tail should be short and very furry with a good plume.

The Blue-Cream is the result of crossing a Blue with a Cream Longhair. This breed was recognized in Britain only 60 years ago.

FURTHER INFORMATION

• The genetic make-up of the Blue-Cream is linked to the Tortoiseshell, with the result that the few males produced are nearly always sterile.

The official mouser at 10 Downing Street for fifteen years was Wilberforce. He was a gift to Edward Heath from the RSPCA, and retired from government service in 1988. Mrs Thatcher's farewell gift to him was a can of pilchards purchased by her from a Moscow supermarket.

Chinchilla Longhair

BREED BASICS

Varieties: Shaded Silver, Golden Persian.
Colours: Snow white coat tipped with black: slightly more black tipping on the Shaded Silver. Golden apricot coat tipped with black or seal brown.
Coat Length: Very long. **Type of Fur:** Fine and silky guard hairs over a dense woolly undercoat.
Markings: Black tipping. **Size:** Medium.
Characteristics: A strong, cobby body with short thick legs. The paw pads should be black or dark brown. The head is round with a short snub brick-red nose and large, rounded green eyes outlined in black. The ears are short with round tips. The whiskers should be long. The tail should be short and very furry with a good plume.

The Chinchilla Longhair is a cat with extravagantly good looks. In the UK, it tends to be less stocky than its American counterpart, with a somewhat longer nose, but both standards call for a cat with an exceptionally beautiful coat. Chinchillas have a reputation for being slightly temperamental.

FURTHER INFORMATION

• Silver tabbies were used to develop this breed, which is one of the earliest, being established since the 1890s. The coat colour has become paler since the early days.

The saying 'A cat may look at a king' dates from 1546 when it appeared in John Heywood's collection of proverbs, published in London.

Cameo Longhair

BREED BASICS

Varieties: Shell, Shaded, Smoke.
Colours: Red, Cream, and Tortie are acceptable in each of the varieties. **Coat Length:** Long.
Type of Fur: Fine and silky guard hairs over a dense woolly undercoat. **Markings:** Coloured tips on white undercoat. **Size:** Medium. **Characteristics:** A strong, cobby body with short thick legs. The paw pads should be pink. The head is round with a short snub pink nose and large, rounded orange or copper-coloured eyes. The ears are short with round tips. The whiskers should be long. The tail should be short and very furry with a good plume.

Cameos have tipped fur, and are somewhat similar to Chinchilla and Smoke Longhairs. There are three densities of tipping – shell, shaded and smoke – depending on how much colour appears on each strand of hair. Shell Cameos have just the smallest amount of colour at the tip of each hair; Shaded Cameos have pigmentation further down the hair shaft and Smoke Cameos only reveal the white undercoat when they move.

FURTHER INFORMATION

• The Cameo colouring is relatively new, and was created by crossing Tortoiseshell and Smoke Longhairs. Darker colouring should appear on the face, down the back and on the legs and feet only.

According to *Cat Fancy*, the most popular name for female cats in the USA are: Samantha, Misty, Muffin, Fluffy, Patches, Pumpkin, Missy, Tabitha and Tigger.

Smoke Longhair

BREED BASICS

Varieties: Black, Blue, Chocolate, Lilac, Red, Tortie, Cream, Blue-Cream, Chocolate Tortie, Lilac Tortie.

Colours: Colour tipping on pale undercoat colour.

Coat Length: Long. **Type of Fur:** Fine and silky guard hairs over a dense woolly undercoat.

Markings: The tipping should be darker on the back, face, feet and legs. On the Tortie Smoke, the face and feet should be a solid colour, preferably with a red or cream facial blaze. **Size:** Medium.

Characteristics: A strong, cobby body with short thick legs. The paw pads should be black on the darker colours and cream on the lighter colours. The head is round with a short snub nose coloured to match the coat, and large, rounded orange or copper-coloured eyes. The ears are short with round tips. The whiskers should be long. The tail should be short and very furry with a good plume.

Smokes have gorgeous coats, with only the very base of each hair showing a pale colour. They can look like solids until the animal moves or the fur is ruffled. They were originally bred in the 1860s by crossing a Chinchilla with a Black Longhair, but now there are several colours.

FURTHER INFORMATION

• Brushing warm bran into the coat of a Longhair helps to keep the fur in good condition. The bran should be hand-warm, and should be carefully brushed out, leaving none behind. This helps to keep the fur clean and lustrous.

Sir Isaac Newton, the English mathematician famous for formulating the law of gravity, may have been the first person to use a cat flap. He had a cat-sized hole cut in the door of his study so that his cat and her

Bi-colour Longhair

BREED BASICS

Varieties: Any solid colour plus white.
Coat Length: Long. **Type of Fur:** Fine and silky guard hairs over a dense woolly undercoat.
Markings: Coloured patches on white background should be solid and evenly distributed, with the white covering a maximum of half the body and the coloured patches up to two-thirds of the body.
Size: Medium. **Characteristics:** A strong, cobby body with short thick legs. The paw pads should match the coat colour. The head is round with a short snub nose coloured to match the coat, and large, rounded copper-coloured eyes. The ears are short with round tips. The whiskers should be long. The tail should be short and very furry with a good plume.

These cats have two-tone coats, which may be of any colour mixed with white. As with any white cat, Bi-colours may need bathing occasionally to keep their coats glistening. At shows Bi-colours were originally grouped together in the 'Any Other Colours' classification, but in the 1960s they were given their own class. The early standard called for exactly symmetrical markings, but this has been relaxed as it has proved too difficult to achieve. Bi-colours have the good nature and placid disposition of most Longhairs.

FURTHER INFORMATION

• Longhairs should be brushed and groomed every day, not only to keep the coat in peak condition, but also to minimize the number of hairs which the cat swallows when grooming himself. The long, fine hairs can cause intestinal and respiratory problems as well as the more common, harmless, fur balls.

Tabby Longhair

BREED BASICS

Varieties/Colours: Brown, Red, Silver, Blue, Cream, Chocolate, Lilac, and four colours of Tortie-tabby (Torbie). **Coat Length:** Long. **Type of Fur:** Fine and silky guard hairs over a dense woolly undercoat. **Markings:** The recognized markings of the Classic, the Mackerel and the Patched Tabby. **Size:** Medium. **Characteristics:** A strong, cobby body with short thick legs. The paw pads should match the coat colour. The head is round with a short snub nose coloured to match the coat, and large, rounded copper-coloured eyes. In the Silver Tabby the eye colour can also be green or hazel. The ears are short with round tips. The whiskers should be long. The tail should be short and very furry with a good plume.

Tabby Longhairs first appeared in Europe in the 17th century and are probably the oldest variety of Persian cat. They were very popular at the end of the 19th century, when the modern standards emerged. Since then the original colour, Brown, has been joined by nine others, but because of the Longhair's luxuriant coat it can sometimes be difficult to distinguish the tabby markings. Brown Classic Tabbies are rather rare.

FURTHER INFORMATION

• Only the original tabby colours of brown, red and silver are universally recognized. The newer colours are not universally accepted.

• Raymond Chandler owned a Longhair called Taki. He called her 'his secretary' because she used often to sit on his manuscripts as he worked.

Tortoiseshell Longhair

BREED BASICS

Varieties: UK – Cameos; USA – Shaded.
Colours: Patched selection of red, cream and black, or of blue, chocolate and lilac. **Coat Length:** Long. **Type of Fur:** Fine and silky guard hairs over a dense woolly undercoat. **Markings:** Colour patches should be evenly distributed. A red or cream facial blaze is desirable. **Size:** Medium. **Country of Origin:** Great Britain. **Characteristics:** A strong, cobby body with short thick legs. The paw pads should be pink or black. The head is round with a short snub nose coloured to match the coat, and large, rounded copper-coloured eyes. The ears are short with round tips. The whiskers should be long. The tail should be short and very furry with a good plume.

The Tortoiseshell Longhair was created from an accidental mating of a pedigree Longhair with non-pedigree Tortoiseshell Shorthair, and has been popular since the turn of the century. As with all tortoiseshell cats, the few males born are generally sterile. Tortoiseshell Longhairs are as friendly and agreeable as all other Longhairs.

FURTHER INFORMATION

• It is not easy to breed cats with good colouration.

Cardinal Richelieu, the power behind the throne of King Louis XIII of France, left pensions to his fourteen cats.

Tortoiseshell and White Longhair

BREED BASICS

Varieties/Colours: White with red, black and cream; or white with blue, chocolate and lilac.
Coat Length: Long. **Type of Fur:** Fine and silky guard hairs over a dense woolly undercoat. **Markings:** In the USA, more white is required, especially on the stomach. In the UK, the white and regular tortoiseshell colours should be evenly distributed. A facial blaze is desirable. **Size:** Medium.

Characteristics: A strong, cobby body with short thick legs. The paw pads should be of broken colour. The head is round with a short snub nose coloured to match the coat, and large, rounded copper-coloured eyes. The ears are short with round tips. The whiskers should be long. The tail should be short and very furry with a good plume.

This breed is known in the USA as the Calico because of the smudges of white intermingled with the tortoiseshell pattern. As usual with tortoiseshells, they are generally female. The best results are usually obtained from including Bi-colours in the mating pattern.

FURTHER INFORMATION

Stephens Island in New Zealand was home to the Stephens Island Wren, a species of flightless bird found nowhere else on earth. When a lighthouse was built on the island in the 19th century, the keeper's cat was single-handedly responsible for exterminating the species. The New Zealand *Canterbury Press* reported, 'The English scientific world will hear simultaneously of its discovery and its disappearance.'

Pewter Longhair

BREED BASICS
Varieties: None. **Colours:** White with black shading.
Coat Length: Long. **Type of Fur:** Fine and silky guard
hairs over a dense woolly undercoat.
Markings: Darker shading on legs and back.
Size: Medium. **Characteristics:** A strong, cobby body
with short thick legs. The paw pads should be
brick-red. The head is round with a short snub nose,
brick-red in colour and outlined in black, and large,
rounded orange or copper-coloured eyes with black
eye rims. The ears are short with round tips. The
whiskers should be long. The tail should be short and
very furry with a good plume.

Like the Chinchilla, the Pewter has a tipped coat, but
with much more density of colour. This breed is
probably the result of mating a Chinchilla with any of
the self-coloured Longhairs.

FURTHER INFORMATION
• The Pewter Longhair is a relatively new breed and,
although at first glance these cats look very similar to
Silver Shaded Longhairs, their golden-coloured eyes
distinguish them.

The first settlers in Australia took the rabbit with
them and before long rabbits had become a plague.

So cats were released to try to control the rabbit. Now cats are understood to be a significant threat to the native wildlife, and opinion is strongly divided over whether cats should or should not still be allowed as pets.

Lilac Longhair

BREED BASICS
Varieties: None. **Coat Length:** Long.
Type of Fur: Fine and silky guard hairs over a dense woolly undercoat. **Markings:** None. **Size:** Medium.
Characteristics: A strong, cobby body with short thick legs. The paw pads should match the coat colour. The head is round with a short snub nose, matching the coat in colour, and large, rounded copper-coloured eyes with black eye rims. The ears are short with round tips. The whiskers should be long. The tail should be short and very furry with a good plume.

Breeders are constantly trying to develop new colours in the coats of these luxurious cats. The Lilac is the dilute form of the Chocolate Longhair, and breeders are still working on developing the colour, which should be pinkish dove-grey.

FURTHER INFORMATION

Cats have 120° of binocular (straight ahead) vision, plus a further 80° to either side. A special membrane at the back of the eye called the *tapetum lucidum* enables cats to make the most of any light.

Chocolate Longhair

BREED BASICS

Varieties: None. **Coat Length:** Long.
Type of Fur: Fine and silky guard hairs over a dense woolly undercoat. **Markings:** None, colour should be solid medium to dark brown. **Size:** Medium.
Characteristics: A strong, cobby body with short thick legs. The paw pads should be brown. The head is round with a short snub nose, brown in colour, and large, rounded copper-coloured eyes with black eye rims. The ears are short with round tips. The whiskers should be long. The tail should be short and very furry with a good plume.

The Chocolate is another newer colour, the first example having been exhibited in 1961. It has not been an easy colour to create, and Havana cats were used in the breeding programme. This resulted in cats with physical characteristics such as a long nose and ears that were not considered desirable, and it has taken some years to breed them out.

FURTHER INFORMATION

The average cat weighs about 5kg/9lb and stands about 31cm/12in high at the shoulder. Cats have 245 bones and 517 muscles, the strongest of which are in the neck and shoulders, and in the hind legs and lumbar region.

The White House has frequently accommodated a first cat. Abraham Lincoln brought the first. Calvin Coolidge had three cats; John F. Kennedy brought the family cat, Tom Kitten. Gerald Ford's cat was a pedigree Siamese; Bill Clinton's daughter Chelsea owns a black and white non-pedigree.

~ COMPENDIUM ~

Choosing and
Caring for your Cat

Will you choose your cat, or will your cat choose you? Many a moggie has simply moved in to a house it has liked the look of! But if you take a decision to become a cat owner, you should ask yourself what kind of cat you want – a pedigree animal, with all its requirements in terms of time and cost, or a non-pedigree? A male or a female? It is not usually a good idea to get a kitten from a pet shop; try a recommended breeder for a pedigree cat, or a humane society for a moggie needing a good home.

FURTHER INFORMATION

• You should check a kitten over carefully for any signs of fleas.

• Look inside the ears for any build-up of dirt or mites.

• Check under the tail to make sure it is clean and dry with no signs of diarrhoea.

• Check that its eyes and mouth are clear and clean.

• The kitten's general demeanour should be alert and playful. If it is quiet and shy it may not be completely well.

• Don't take a kitten away from its mother until it is at least eight weeks old. Pedigree cats in the UK cannot be sold until they are twelve weeks old.

- If you are buying a pedigree cat, always get expert advice.
- Always have your kitten innoculated against feline enteritis and feline influenza, and don't be tempted to neglect the annual booster shots.

Unless you are planning to breed from your cat, it is a good idea to have it neutered. Entire tom cats will spray to mark their territory, and the smell is extremely disagreeable. An unspayed female cat will present you with a succession of kittens unless you keep her permanently indoors; and will make a lot of noise when she comes into season.

When you collect your new cat, transport it to its new home in a good strong container. Allow it plenty of time to settle in; if it is an adult cat, try to bring something familiar with it, such as its blanket. Keep your cat indoors for about a week, and spend time playing with it and spoiling it. Handle a kitten frequently, but very carefully. Cats are naturally clean and fastidious and are fairly easy to house train, but be patient and calm. Most cats pick up the use of a cat flap without too much difficulty, and you can then do without a litter tray in the house. Exercise is not usually necessary for cats, who spend a great deal of time asleep. But if you have a longhaired cat you will have to spend at least 15 minutes a day grooming it. If your cat gets very dirty you could consider giving it a bath, but most cats hate water and may show displeasure!

FURTHER INFORMATION
• The basic equipment you will need is a litter tray and a supply of fresh litter; feeding and water bowls; an elasticated collar with a bell if you want to discourage your cat from catching birds; and grooming brushes.
• Your cat will probably find its own favourite sleeping place, but lots of cats like a special bed or beanbag.

- Cats should always have fresh water available, but don't worry if your cat seems not to drink much. Cats have very efficient kidneys and can obtain much of the water they need from foods such as meat and gravy or fresh fish.
- Cats are carnivores and cannot be fed on a vegetarian diet. Give two meals a day (three or four to kittens) of either canned food, or semi-moist food in a foil pack, or dry food from a packet, or freshly cooked meat or fish. Many cats will feed as they need to from a bowl of dry food left out all the time.
- Many house plants are dangerous to cats, among them laurel, poinsettia and true ivy.
- Cats like to chew grass, which helps them to bring up any fur balls. If your cat can't go outside, you might like to grow a window box of grass at home.

Healthcare

Cats are generally a very healthy species, with strong flexible bodies and robust systems, but as with all animals, they can have health problems. One of the first things to do when you get your cat is to find a good vet – before you need one. It may also be a good idea to consider health insurance, as veterinary care can be expensive, and there is no National Health for cats. If your cat has not been vaccinated against feline infectious enteritis and feline influenza, this should be your first priority. These two illnesses are very infectious and can be extremely serious, but an annual booster jab will keep them at bay.

FURTHER INFORMATION

• Feline enteritis is caused by a virus which attacks the bowels and central nervous system. Symptoms are the cat seeming generally unwell, and there may be vomiting. It is often fatal if it takes hold.

• Feline influenza describes two viruses which attack the upper respiratory tract, which will cause your cat to cough and sneeze.

• There is a vaccine now available against feline leukaemia, and another against chlamydia.

• There is also a vaccination available for rabies, an illness which is always fatal if it is not caught in time. In the UK there are quarantine laws which are strictly enforced to stop the spread of the disease. UK animals are not vaccinated against rabies.

• Cats can also catch the feline equivalent of AIDS – but this is not under any circumstances transmittable to humans.

• Cats may also suffer from other illnesses such as arthritis, asthma and diabetes amongst others.

Cats, in particular those which spend plenty of time out of doors, often suffer from parasites, both internal and external. The first sign is usually the cat scratching more than usual, but you may also see bald patches in the fur, and wet or dry sore places. The most common problem is an infestation of fleas, and these, together with other skin parasites such as ticks, lice, and mange mites, are much more common in hot weather. Fleas live not only on the cat itself but also in the cat's favourite bedding, in carpets and in upholstery, so when you treat the cat for fleas you should also treat your soft furnishings.

FURTHER INFORMATION

• Most remedies bought over the counter for skin parasites are not nearly as effective as a preparation given by the vet, and it is probably worthwhile paying what will be slightly more for something which will really work.

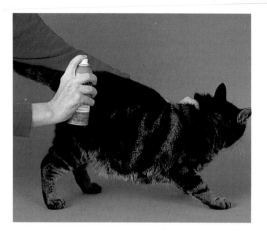

- In order to check whether your cat has fleas – you may not be able to see the actual insects – stand the cat on a piece of damp white paper and run a comb through the fur. If this produces a scattering of fine black dust-like particles, and if the particles turn red on contact with the damp paper, there are fleas: you have just combed out some of the droppings, which are mainly composed of blood.
- Many cats suffer at one time or another from worms, either roundworms or tapeworms. Worming drugs, available from your vet, are safe and effective.
- Ringworm, despite its name, is actually a fungal infection, and can be treated by drugs.

Cats can suffer from a wide range of ailments, such as constipation, diarrhoea, dandruff, bronchitis and pleurisy. Take your cat to the vet immediately if you suspect it may be unwell. Keep a careful eye on your cat's health and you should be able to detect symptoms before they become serious. You should check your cat's mouth, ears and eyes regularly for any signs of trouble. Teeth should be white and clean-looking, with no sign of a build-up of brownish plaque or bad smell, and of course teeth should not be loose. The tongue should be pale pink and clear. Eyes should be bright and alert. Cats have a 'third eyelid' called a 'haw' which is

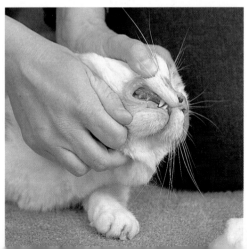

sometimes visible at the inside corners of the eye. If this remains visible for more than a day or so it may indicate that something is wrong, and you should consult the vet.

FURTHER INFORMATION

• If your cat has trouble with its ears you will probably know because it scratches more than usual, or shakes its head frequently. Check with your vet, who may pour a little paraffin oil, warmed to body heat, into the ear, to provide relief. Don't try this on your own, for ear troubles can have many causes and it is best not to tamper.

The most common accidents to befall cats are accidents on the road. Moving the injured cat as little as possible, try to get it onto a sheet or coat, and take it as fast as possible to the vet.

Falls are also common, and cats do not always land safely. Fractured jaws are more common than fractured limbs because the cat's head may hit the ground. Keep the cat as quiet as possible and rush it to the vet.

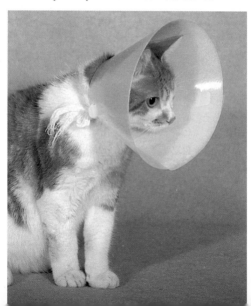

Cats can be poisoned by eating or drinking a noxious substance, or by licking it off its fur. Symptoms include vomiting, convulsions and collapse. Don't try to induce vomiting unless you are sure the poison was not caustic, and take a specimen of the poison to the vet with you if you can.

You can give first aid yourself for some problems. If your cat has been in a fight or cut itself while out, you should gently disinfect the wound (make sure your disinfectant is suitable for cats) and check to make sure no abscess forms. If the cat is bleeding, apply gentle pressure to stop the bleeding, clean the wound and bandage carefully. Only surface wounds should be treated at home. For anything serious see your vet.

For a burn, run the burned area under cold running water for a considerable time, and then take the cat to the vet.

It can be difficult to deal with splinters and insect stings at home as the cat will often not stay still enough to allow you to pull these out. The vet will be able to do this for you.

FURTHER INFORMATION

- A basic first aid kit might contain:
  Cat disinfectant
  Antiseptic cream and lotion
  Bandages
  Round-ended scissors
  Cotton wool
  Lint gauze

Psychology

Cats seem to fit in especially well with modern urban living. Although they seldom respond to training like a dog or a horse, they provide today's busy, apartment-dwelling professionals with company and affection; yet they are generally undemanding, relatively cheap to feed, and do not require the investment of time and energy that most dogs demand. They appear to find it possible to remain basically self-sufficient, while at the same time enjoying the comforts the human home can provide.

Cats are not truly social animals; of all the cat family only lions operate as a group – and indeed there is no collective noun for cats. So while dogs fit into a human household taking their place in a hierarchy which would be familiar in a pack, cats fit in a slightly different way. When a kitten is taken from its mother and homed with humans, it will regard the humans as its mother. Humans offer a safe lair, security from enemies and competitors, food on demand. Cats can have comfortable reminders of kittenhood, with a warm lap to curl up on, and memories of suckling days when it kneads soft fabric with its paws, as it did to stimulate the flow of its mother's milk.

Out in the garden the cat will still be a hunter, maybe with a territory to defend. At home he can be an infant.

However, even though cats have retained their integrity on the whole, modern living can present some

traumas which may give rise to behavioural problems. The most common of these are spraying and soiling indoors, biting and other aggressive behaviour; but more bizarre examples of problem behaviour include eating fabric (including rubber), projectile vomiting, and self-mutilation.

The point at which behaviour becomes a problem depends on the tolerance level of the owner and the level of his dependency on his pet, but the first port of call is usually the vet. Once the possibility of illness has been eliminated, the vet may refer the cat and its owner to a specialist in cat psychology and behaviour problems.

Cats in the Arts

Literature

There are probably more cats in literature than any other animal. Fables and stories abound in every language and from every culture, from Russia to China, from Arabia to Africa. Children learning to read are taught that 'C is for Cat', and that 'the cat sat on the mat'. In the playground they chant 'Ding dong bell, pussy's in the well' and 'Pussy cat, pussy cat, where have you been? I've been up to London to visit the queen.' Later they read Kathleen Hart's stories about Orlando the Marmalade Cat, and Beatrix Potter's Tale of Tom Kitten. Adults too love Edward Lear's The Owl and the Pussycat, and the Cheshire Cat from Alice's Adventures in Wonderland needs no introduction. Many of Aesop's fables and Grimms' fairy tales feature cats.

FELINE FACTS

• Many of the world's great poets have written about cats. Chaucer featured a cat in The Manciple's Tale; Thomas Hood, D. H. Lawrence, Wordsworth, Keats, Walter de la Mare and Christina Rossetti are among those who have written poems about cats sleeping, washing, playing. W. B. Yeats' The Cat and the Moon is one of the most lyrical: 'Minnaloushe creeps through the grass/Alone, important and wise,/And lifts to the changing moon/His changing eyes'. Thomas Gray, the

18th century English poet, wrote an Ode on the death of a favourite cat, drowned in a tub of gold fish. Rum Tum Tugger, Bustopher Jones, Mr Mistoffelees and the others from T. S. Eliot's *Old Possum's Book of Practical Cats* have been given a new lease of life by the musical *Cats*. And Don Marquis, the Chicago poet, has written about the unforgettable Mehitabel, who was 'tourjours gai', and his cockroach friend, Archy. Christopher Smart, the 18th century English poet who died insane, wrote *On Jeoffry, My Cat:*

'For I will consider my Cat Jeoffry…
For there is nothing sweeter than his peace when at rest.
For there is nothing brisker than his life
when in motion…'

• Cats have starred in many novels and short stories. Saki's *Tobermory* features a cat who learns to talk, a skill which causes consternation among his owner's house-guests who realize the indiscretions he will have witnessed. Edgar Allen Poe wrote many stories featuring cats, perhaps most famously the macabre *The Black Cat*. Paul Gallico's *The Silent Meow, Thomasina* and *Jennie* will always be firm favourites, but perhaps the best description of a cat comes from Rudyard Kipling's *Just So Stories,* published in 1902. *The Cat that Walked by Himself* describes how he 'will kill mice and he will be kind to Babies when he is in the house, just as long as they do not pull his tail too hard. But when he has done that, and between times, and when the moon gets up and night comes, he is the Cat that walks by himself, and all places are alike to him. Then he goes out to the Wet Wild Woods or up the Wet Wild Trees or on the Wet Wild Roofs, waving his tail and walking by his wild lone.'

'Please would you tell me,' said Alice a little timidly ... 'why your cat grins like that? 'It's a Cheshire cat, said the Duchess, 'and that's why.' ... The Cat only grinned when it saw Alice. It looked good-natured, she thought: still it had *very* long claws and a great many teeth, so she felt that it ought to be treated with respect.

Alice's Adventures in Wonderland by Lewis Carroll

Art

The very earliest pictures of cats are probably those painted on the walls of ancient Egyptian tombs, where the cat was sacred and associated with the goddess Bastet. In the East exquisite paintings of cats were made on silk scrolls in China around the time of the Ming Dynasty, and artists depicted cats in their paintings in Japan, India, and Korea. In the West, from around the 10th century, cats were regarded with fear as manifestations of the devil, and artists such as Cellini working in the 16th century would show a cat at the feet of Judas to emphasize its link with evil. Leonardo da Vinci, however, said, 'The smallest feline is a masterpiece', and drew many flawless studies of cats. George Stubbs, the celebrated horse artist, painted the great thoroughbred, Godolphin Arabian, with its friend, a cat. In 1809, John Lawrence described how the little

black cat became inseparable from the great racehorse, and pined to death when he died.

FELINE FACTS

• Louis Wain, the English artist who died insane in 1939, is famous for his cat pictures. He painted highly idiosyncratic pictures of cats, often dressed in clothes and engaged in a wide range of human situations: playing cricket, having a tea party, boating, in the schoolroom.

• Edouard Manet and Renoir both enjoyed painting cats. Gwen John, the English painter and sister of Augustus John, painted a charming Sketch of a Seated Cat. Other more modern artists well known for their paintings of cats include the American artists Andy Warhol and Will Barnett. Today one of the best known painter of cats is Lesley Anne Ivory, whose delightful paintings are to be found on a wide variety of books and merchandise.

Cartoon

Cats are perennial favourites in the world of cartoons, both on film and in books or comics. Tom and Jerry made their debut in 1940, with Hanna Barbera making 113 cartoon shorts, and another team of producers a further 47. Tom and Jerry collected seven Oscars during their career. Sylvester was at his most popular during the 1940s and 1950s, though cartoons featuring his pursuit of Tweety Pie are still in vogue today. The Pink Panther first appeared, to the music of Henry Mancini, in the opening credits of Peter Sellers' 1964 film The Pink Panther. In the film the Pink Panther was actually a diamond, but the cartoon Panther was an immediate hit and by 1984 had starred in some 95 cartoon shorts, TV shows, and in comic books. Top Cat, the street-wise alley cat, starred in 28 episodes of a TV show, starting in 1961, and to this day enjoys a cult following.

FELINE FACTS

• Walt Disney is responsible for several of our favourite cartoon cats. Figaro, the little black and white kitten, appeared in the 1940 film Pinocchio, and the fat, wicked Lucifer appeared in Cinderella in 1950. The last movie Disney authorized before his death was The Aristocats, which appeared in 1970, and which has become a firm favourite. The voice of the mama cat, Duchess, was provided by Eva Gabor.

• Perhaps the most famous cartoon cat today is Jim

Davis's Garfield. Garfield was created in 1978, and has gone on to capture the hearts of the world. He runs in over 2000 different newspapers worldwide, the strip is translated into twelve different languages, and Garfield has a TV show as well. Garfield's fans can quote his bon mots, such as 'Big, fat, hairy deal!', and know that his favourite food is lasagna and that he can't start the day without coffee.

Film and Opera

Although cats are not as easy to train as dogs, it is possible for a cat to be taught how to do tricks. Perhaps the earliest cat film-star was Pyewacket, who starred with James Stewart, Jack Lemmon and Kim Novak in the 1958 film *Bell, Book and Candle.* Audrey Hepburn, as the kooky Holly Golightly in *Breakfast at Tiffany's,* had a cat simply called Cat. Cat was played by Orangey, a star who won an award for his role in this 1961 film. Disney's *The Cat from Outer Space* featured an extra-terrestrial cat called Jake who commands a spaceship forced to land on earth for repairs. And Stephen King's *Cat's Eye,* filmed in 1985, required several cats to take it in turns to play the main role.

FELINE FACTS

• Sheila Burnford's book *The Incredible Journey* was animated by the Walt Disney studios in 1963. It was the true story of a Siamese cat, a bull terrier and a Labrador who were left behind when their owners moved house, and who made their way over 200 miles of Canada to find their way safely home. The film has been re-released many times since its first screening.

• *L'Enfant et les Sortilèges* is a famous opera by Ravel, based on a story written for children by Sidonie-Gabrielle Colette (1873-1954). Not only does it contain a duet for a male and a female cat, but dancing too. It is a charming, lyrical fantasy on the loves of cats.

Famous Cats

Cats are the heroes of many a fable and story – Dick Whittington's cat and Puss-in-Boots were both resourceful, clever creatures without whom their humans would not have flourished – but many real life cats are famous too. Queen Victoria owned Persian cats, and because of her royal patronage the popularity of the Persian cat increased by leaps and bounds. Her cat White Heather lived on long after the Queen's death in 1901, cared for and fed by the palace staff. The British Museum was home to a black cat called Mike, well-known to all the staff and many visitors. When he died in 1929 an obituary was published, and poems were written to his memory.

Maybe the most famous feline television star in England is Arthur, the white cat who had been trained to help himself to food from the tin with his paw, and who advertised pet food so successfully that the manufacturers renamed the food after the cat himself, calling it Arthur's. Arthur has now retired from television work, but he is still a star, with a mail-order catalogue to his name, a biography published, and a trophy named after him, the Arthur Award, which is a sort of feline Oscar.

FELINE FACTS

• Puss in Boots first appeared in Giovanni Francesco Straparola's book of fables, but it was Charles Perrault's version, written in France in 1696, which has become famous.

• A cat called Mousam was instructed to report for jury duty. He was eventually disqualified on the grounds that he could not speak English!

• Dr Samuel Johnson's pampered cat Hodge was immortalised by James Boswell, who tells in his Life of Johnson how the doctor used to indulge his cat, even going out himself to purchase Hodge's favourite oysters rather than send a servant.

• Theophile Gautier, the French novelist, had a cat named Eponine, who used to dine at table with him. She would sit on a chair, resting her forepaws on the table, and eat each course of the dinner from soup to dessert.

Cat Lore

There are more superstitions and myths surrounding cats than any other animal, perhaps reflecting their mysterious and enigmatic nature.

• Black cats. Perhaps the most ardently-held belief is that black cats are lucky – though the belief is turned on its head in the United States, where black cats are considered unlucky. The European belief that a black cat could bring good luck might derive from medieval days, when cats, and particularly black cats, were thought to be manifestations of Satan. If a black cat crossed one's path and no harm befell one, this was obviously extremely lucky! Black cats are closely associated with the occult and today are symbols associated with Hallowe'en.

• A cat has nine lives. Nine used to be considered a lucky number, being thrice times three, so it was deemed a suitable number of lives for cats, which so often seem able to escape the most difficult of situations. It is also said that the prophet Mohammed touched his cat three times, giving him three times three lives.

• White cats make bad mothers. White cats are often deaf, owing to a genetically linked fault which causes irreversible damage to the inner ear, so a white cat cannot hear her kittens calling and will seem to ignore them. However, white cats are usually extra-sensitive to vibrations, and seem otherwise to cope well with the disability.

• Cats have ESP. They do not have ESP, but as hunters they are certainly highly attuned to sounds and sensations that humans cannot perceive. Their sensitive whiskers and acute hearing and vision allow cats to apprehend changes in static electricity and air pressure as well as to smell rain, to hear sounds beyond the reach of human ears, and to see quite well in much dimmer light than humans can.

• Cat's cradle. This children's game of looped string may originate in an Eastern European custom, in which a cat would be secured in a cradle and rocked in the presence of a newly-wed couple to encourage a pregnancy – cats having been for centuries symbols of fertility.

• Let the cat out of the bag. To let the cat out of the bag is to give away a secret. The saying probably arises from the days when one might wish to purchase a piglet at market. Tricksters would try to sell a sack which actually contained a cat rather than a valuable piglet. If the cat struggled hard and got out of the sack, the secret was out.

Cat Names

The naming of a cat is a serious matter, as T. S. Eliot, the English poet, recognized in his Old Possum's Book of Practical Cats. He felt that a cat should have three different names: one to be the family's everyday name; another to be 'a name that's particular' – and his suggestions include Quaxo and Coricopat; and thirdly 'the name that no human research can discover'. This is the name that an inscrutable cat has chosen for itself. The names in Old Possum include Bustopher Jones, Skimbleshanks, and Rumpleteazer.

• Many people give their cats more than one name. Pedigree cats will usually have a 'name that's particular' as well as the name by which its family calls it.

• People with two cats often bestow complementary names on their animals, such as Orlando and Grace, or Bonnie and Clyde.

• Some of the most popular names for cats are Tigger, Fluffy, Blackie, Ginger, and Stripey.

• The poet Robert Southey christened his cat the most noble the Archduke Rumpelstiltzchen, Marquis Macbum, Earl Tomlefnagne, Barin Raticide, Waowhler, and Skaratch; Rumpel for short.

• Marilyn Monroe's cat was called Mitsou.

• The American writer Mark Twain called his cat Beelzebub, apparently because he wanted to teach his children how to say this difficult word.

• The English poet Thomas Hood's cat was called Tabitha Longclaws Tiddleywinks, and her three kittens were Pepperpot, Scratchaway and Sootikins.

• The prophet Mohammed called his favourite cat
Muezza. It is said that, on finding Muezza asleep on his
arm, Mohammed cut off his sleeve rather than
disturb the cat.

• Charles Dickens' cat, Wilhelmina, was wont to put
out the candle with her paw if she was not given
enough attention.

Glossary

Agouti In the tabby, where the coat is flecked it is called agouti. Here the hairs are banded with yellow. Where the yellow bands are missing the coat is black (non-agouti).

Albino Any animal with no pigment in skin or hair, appearing totally white with pinkish eyes.

Awn hairs Short, coarse hairs lying underneath the cat's top coat.

Barring Striped pattern found in tabbies, but considered a fault in self-coloured cats.

Bi-colour Cat with patches of white and one solid colour.

Bloodline A cat's ancestry, showing cats related to one another often by their pedigree.

Breed Cats with a similar appearance based on a defined standard.

Calico American word for Tortoiseshell and White colouring.

Calling The distinctive sound made by a female cat on heat.

Cameo Hair with red or cream tipping.

Camouflage Colouring or marking which allows an animal to blend in with its surroundings.

Carnivore An animal which eats meat.

Carpal pad Special pads found above the cat's front feet which help to absorb impact on landing.

Cat Fancy The organization and selected breeding and showing of cats.

Cattery A place where cats can board or where they are bred.

Classification A system of grouping living things according to characteristics they share.

Champion Title awarded to a cat after a number of wins at a show.

Chromosome Structures present in nuclei of cells carrying genetic information.

Cobby Short, compact body shape of cats.

Congenital Health difficulty arising before birth but not hereditary.

Cross-breeding Breeding between two different breeds.

Dilute Pale version of a colour.

Dominant characteristic A genetic characteristic imparted by a parent to its kitten.

Double coat Short soft undercoat with a longer outer coat.

Down hair Short, soft secondary hairs.

Ear furnishings Hair growing within the ear.

Entire Not neutered.

Feral Domestic cat which has come to live wild.

Flehmening Facial expression a cat makes when it draws scent over the Jacobsen's organ in the roof of its mouth.

Genes Determine the characteristic of the animal and are inherited in pairs, one from each parent.

GCCF Governing Council of the Cat Fancy (UK).

Guard hairs Long hairs forming the outer coat.

Heat Female cat's period of oestrus.

Himalayan patterning Darker colour at extremities of the body, often affected by temperature.

In-breeding Mating of close relatives, sometimes leading to genetic mutations in kittens.

Kink Bend in the tail usually of Siamese or other Oriental cats.

Level bite Jaws aligned with no overlap.

Litter All kittens born in a single birth. Also the contents of a dirt tray.

Melanin Dark pigmentation.

Mittens White fur on front feet.

Moggy Slang term for a non-pedigree cat.

Moult Shedding of fur, usually seasonal.

Mutation Genetic change causing a difference in appearance from the parents. Can be unhealthy or harmless.

Neuter Cat which has been castrated (male) or spayed (female).

Nictating membrane Also known as the haw or third eyelid, thin membrane visible at inner corners of a cat's eyes at times of ill health.

Nocturnal Active at night.

Nose leather Skin of nose pad.

Odd-eyed Eyes of different colour, often blue and orange.

Oestrus Breeding time for female cats.

Out-cross Mating with unrelated cat, possibly not of same breed.

Pads Cushions without fur on underside of cat's feet.

Papillae Tiny hooks on cat's tongue which give the tongue its roughness.

Pedigree Written record of the family of a pure-bred cat.

Points Darker coloured areas of body, usually legs, tail, face and ears.

Polydactyl Cat with more toes than is usual.

Premier Neutered champion.

Queen Unneutered female cat.

Range Area in which a particular cat lives.

Recessive gene Gene passed from generation to generation but not always with a visible result.

Recognition Acceptance of standard for new breed of cat by cat association.

Retractable claws Claws which may be pulled back into sheaths when not in use.

Rustiness Traces of cinnamon colour visible in fur of a black cat.

Sable American description of brown Burmese.

Scarab marking 'M' shaped mark on the forehead of tabbies.

Seal Dark brown coloration typically describing points of Siamese.

Spraying When a cat (usually male) sprays urine to mark its territory.

Squint Cross-eyes.

Standard of points System used by show judges at cat shows.

Stifle Cat's knee joint on hind leg.

Tabby Coat marking which can be striped, spotted, blotched, or full agouti.

Tapetum lucidum Layer of cells at back of cat's eye which reflect light, helping to give good night vision.

Ticking Bands of colour on each hair.

Tipped Coloured ends of hairs.

Tom Unneutered male cat.

Torbie Tortoiseshell Tabby.

Type Overall size and shape of cat.

Undercoat Short soft hairs at base of coat.

Van pattern Coat mainly white, with head and tail coloured.

Wedge-shaped Shape of head of Siamese and similar breeds.

Whiskers Stiff hairs with highly sensitive nerves at the root.

All photographs in this book were taken and supplied by Marc Henrie, ASC, 22 Warbeck Rd, London W12, except:
Pages 80, 81, 132, 133, Paddy Cutts at Animals Unlimited; 89, Larry Johnson Photography; 231, The Owl and The Pussycat illustration © Helen Cooper. Published courtesy of Hamish Hamilton; 235, Alice's Adventures in Wonderland illustration © John Penniel. Published courtesy of Chancellor Press; 234, The Blue Cushion, by Horatio Henry (Bonhams, London) courtesy of The Bridgeman Art Library; 233, Cats, by Julius Asam (Phillips, The International Fine Art Auctioneers) courtesy of The Bridgeman Art Library; 237, Tom and Jerry, courtesy of Turner Entertainment Co., 1995.

Useful addresses

Association of Pet Behaviour
Counsellors,
257 Royal College Street,
London NW1 9LU

The Governing Council of the
Cat Fancy (GCCF)
4-6 Penel Orlieu
Bridgwater
Somerset TA6 3PG

Cat Association of Britain(CA)
Mill House
Letcombe Regis
Oxfordshire OX12 9JD

Fédération Internationale
Feline (FIFe)
Boerhaavelaan 23
NO-5644 BB Eindhoven
Netherlands

Governing Council of the
Associated Cat Clubs
of South Africa
c/o Mrs M. Simpson
45 Edison Drive
Meadowridge 7800
South Africa

British Small Animal
Veterinary Association
Kingsley House, Church Lane
Shurdington, Cheltenham
Gloucestershire GL51 5TQ

American Cat Association (ACA)
8101 Katherine Drive
Panorama City
CA 91402, USA

American Cat Fanciers'
Association (ACFA)
PO Box 203
Point Lookout
MO 65726, USA

Cat Fanciers' Federation (CFF)
9509 Montgomery Road
Cinncinatti
OH 45242, USA

Co-ordinating Cat Council of
Australia (CCCofA)
Box No 4317 GPO, Sydney,
NSW 2001, Australia

British Association of
Homoeopathic Veterinary
Surgeons, Chinham House
Stanford in the Vale, Faringdon
Oxfordshire SN7 8NQ

The Cats' Protection League
17 Kings Road, Horsham
West Sussex RH13 5PP

Feline Advisory Bureau
The Brewery, Church Street,
Tisbury,
Wiltshire SP3 6NH

Index

COLLINS GEM

Bestselling Collins Gem titles include:

Gem English Dictionary (£3.99)

Gem Thesaurus (£3.99)

Gem French Dictionary (£3.99)

Gem German Dictionary (£3.99)

Gem Calorie Counter (£2.99)

Gem Basic Facts Mathematics (£3.50)

Gem SAS Survival Guide (£3.99)

Gem Babies' Names (£2.99)

Gem Card Games (£3.50)

Gem Ready Reference (£3.50)

All Collins Gems are available from your local bookseller or can be ordered directly from the publishers.

In the UK, contact Mail Order, Dept 2A, HarperCollins Publishers, Westerhill Rd, Bishopbriggs, Glasgow, G64 2QT, listing the titles required and enclosing a cheque or p.o. for the value of the books plus £1.00 for the first title and 25p for each additional title to cover p&p. Access and Visa cardholders can order on 0141-772 2281 (24 hr).

In Australia, contact Customer Services, HarperCollins Distribution, Yarrawa Rd, Moss Vale 2577 (tel. [048] 68 0300). **In New Zealand**, contact Customer Services, HarperCollins Publishers, 31 View Rd, Glenfield, Auckland 10 (tel. [09] 444 3740). **In Canada**, contact your local bookshop.

All prices quoted are correct at time of going to press.

COLLINS